TWAYNE'S WORLD AUTHORS SERIES

A Survey of the World's Literature

CHINA

William Schultz, University of Arizona

EDITOR

Pa Chin

TWAS 496

Pa Chin

PA CHIN

By NATHAN K. MAO
Shippensburg State College

TWAYNE PUBLISHERS
A DIVISION OF G. K. HALL & CO., BOSTON

Library of Congress Cataloging in Publication Data

Mao, Nathan K
    Pa Chin.

(Twayne's world author series ; TWAS 496)
Bibliography: p. 161–66
Includes index.
1. Li, Fei-kan, 1905–   —Criticism and interpretation.
I. Title.
PL2780.F4Z826   895.1'3'5   78-6268
ISBN 0-8057-6337-6

29May 81

Dedicated to my Father and to the Memory of my Mother,
Mrs. Mao Wan Kuei-ping (1911–1974)

Contents

About the Author

Born in 1942 in China, Nathan K. Mao was educated at New Asia College, Hong Kong, and at Yale and Wisconsin. He is the translator of Li Yü's *Twelve Towers*, Pa Chin's *Cold Nights*, Chang Hsiao-feng's *The Man of Wu-ling,* the author of *Li Yü,* and the coauthor of *Classical Chinese Fiction: Studies and Bibliographies.* He now teaches English at Shippensburg State College, Shippensburg, Pennsylvania.

Preface

One of the most popular writers of twentieth-century China is Pa Chin, a favorite of both the students and the general public during the 1930s and 1940s. In a survey conducted among Chinese college and high-school students in 1937, he was second only to Lu Hsün as the most popular writer.[1] Reports from Mainland China in 1972 showed that he was then once again a favorite writer of the people, and that many readers ranked his books with such classical Chinese novels as *The Water Margin* and *The Romance of the Three Kingdoms*.[2] In the West, there have been several critical studies of his works: O. Briere's article in 1942, Jean Monsterleet's in the 1940s and 1950s,[3] and Olga Lang's monumental work, *Pa Chin and His Writings,* in 1967. In 1975 he and Mao Tun were nominated for the Nobel Prize in Literature. The nominators, British and French writers, felt that Pa Chin and Mao Tun were the two authors who best reflected social and political life in China prior to the Communist victory in 1949.[4]

Among the studies of Pa Chin, Olga Lang's is the most important, but she emphasizes Pa Chin's work "primarily as a source of Chinese social and intellectual history."[5] While such an approach is justified, it is my purpose to evaluate Pa Chin's major works from the point of view of literary criticism and to examine the techniques he employed as well as the effects achieved by these techniques. It is intended that this book will show both his weaknesses and his strengths as a major Chinese writer of the twentieth century.

My gratitude goes to the late Mr. Sanford Marlow of La Jolla, California, for reading the manuscript and providing useful suggestions, and particularly to Melanie for her patience, understanding, and love.

NATHAN K. MAO

Shippensburg State College

Chronology

1904   Born in Chengtu, Szechwan province.
1907   Family moves to Kuangyüan, northern Szechwan.
1911   Family moves back to Chengtu.
1912   The Republic of China is established.
1914   Mother dies.
1917   Father dies.
1919   Grandfather dies. May Fourth Incident.
1923   Leaves Chengtu for Shanghai.
1925   May Thirtieth Incident.
1927   Leaves for France. Purge of Communists in Shanghai.
1929   Publishes the novel *Destruction*.
1931   Eldest brother commits suicide; publishes the novel *Family* and other works; Japan attacks Manchuria.
1934- Lives in Japan.
1935
1937   The Marco Polo Bridge Incident; Japan massively invades China.
1944   Marries Miss Ch'en Yun-chen in Kweiyang, Kweichow province.
1945   Japan surrenders; elder brother dies.
1949   Communist victory.
1952   Spends seven months in Korea.
1953   Visits Korea again after the Armistice.
1961   Visits Japan.
1962   Visits North Vietnam and Canton. His collected works published in fourteen volumes.
1966   Purged during the Cultural Revolution.
1975   Nominated for the Nobel Prize in Literature.
1977   "Revived" on Mainland China.

CHAPTER 1
Biographical Sketch

I Early Childhood

ON the eve of Pa Chin's birth, the goddess of childbearing appeared to his mother in a dream to inform her that she had been chosen to give birth to a child that had been intended for her sister-in-law, because the gods were afraid that the sister-in-law might not take good care of it.[1] On the next day, November 25, 1904, Pa Chin, whose real name is Li Fei-kan, was born into a traditional upper-class family in Chengtu, Szechwan province, in western China. Pa Chin's grandfather and great-grandfather had both been magistrates, and a few years after his birth, his father assumed a magistrate's position. The huge family, including Pa Chin's parents, uncles, aunts, brothers, sisters, cousins, nieces, and nephews as well as a large number of servants, lived in a traditional family compound under the rule of his grandfather. Of the first few years of Pa Chin's life little is known.

In the second half of 1907, Pa Chin's immediate family moved to Kuang-yüan in northern Szechwan, where his father served as the local magistrate. Together with his parents, two elder sisters, and two elder brothers he lived in the *yamen,* an official walled compound. Fronted by a large unused plot of land and flanked by jails on two sides, the compound's four units were separated from each other by courtyards. Pa Chin's father held court in the first unit, and the other three were living quarters for the family and servants. Life was pleasant for young Pa Chin.

School was undemanding. Every day a mild-mannered tutor taught the basic classics to Pa Chin and other children in a special room. While classes were being held, an elderly gray-haired servant waited on the pupils. After class every afternoon, Pa Chin played in the courtyards with Li Yao-lin, his elder brother, and a thirteen-year-old bondservant. The courtyards were overgrown with tall

13

grass and mulberry trees and filled with chickens. The children
picked mulberries, gave names to the chickens, and played games.

Pa Chin's sentimental mother was the most formative influence
during his early childhood. She taught him and her other children
to appreciate literature, including her favorite poem, "Wang
Chiang-nan" ("Gazing at the South") by Li Yü (937–978):

> So much to regret:
> Last night my soul within a dream
> Seemed again, as in former days, to wander in the
>   imperial gardens,
> Where carriages drifted like flowing water, the horses
>   like dragons;
> And the breath of spring was just upon the moonlit flowers.[2]

She not only loved literature but also life itself. A daughter-in-law
in a traditional family, she had to obey her elders and subordinate
her interests to theirs. But she did not complain, always smiled, and
taught her children the importance of love, the objects of which to
her included the galaxy of stars, the birds, the sun, cats, birds, and
all human beings.[3] It was perhaps due to her influence that Pa Chin
became a sentimentalist too. On one occasion as a child, he
mourned the slaughter of a favorite chicken for a family feast, an
experience which he claimed he never quite forgot.

Pa Chin's compassion for the chicken led him to wonder about
the necessity of corporal punishment for criminals. He often saw
his magistrate father sitting loftily in a chair, interrogating and
sometimes having a recalcitrant criminal tortured to obtain a confession. Through his mother, he asked his father why torture was
needed. Though no satisfactory answer was forthcoming, his
father, Pa Chin remembers, soon discarded the use of torture.

Pa Chin's curiosity led him one day into his sister's room, where
he found and looked through an illustrated edition of the ancient
Lieh-nu chüan (*Biographies of Illustrious Women*). He was fascinated by ancient female attire and puzzled as to why all the women
looked unhappy. He was even more perplexed when he saw pictures
of a woman cutting off her hand, of another burning in a fire, and
of others who were drowning in water and committing suicide,
some with scissors and others with ropes. Wondering why his two
sisters had to read that book, he asked his mother for an explana-
tion. Matter-of-factly she replied that the women in the book were

models for the young because they all had exemplary virtues; for instance, a widow who was so ashamed when her hand was touched by a stranger that she chose to cut it off, and a palace lady-in-waiting who chose to die in the flames, since there was no one available to escort her out of the burning palace, and had she chosen to leave it by herself, it would have been a serious breach of "propriety." In sum, Pa Chin's mother gave him the impression that women must uphold the principles of "propriety" at any cost and must be ready to give up their lives, if necessary, so that their conduct could remain "exemplary" according to traditional tenets. Though Pa Chin loved his mother dearly, he found it difficult to agree with her on this.

Pa Chin and his elder brother, Yao-lin, shared their bedroom with Yang Sao, a woman-servant in her thirties. A neat woman, she forbade the boys to do somersaults in bed or to spit on the floor. Patient and loving, she told them stories of ghosts, knights-errant, and fairy-spirits every night before they went to sleep. She earned their total affection. Pa Chin fondly described that period as "without tears, without sorrow, without anger — only tranquil happiness."[4] But Yang Sao became ill and was separated from the boys and placed in a sparsely furnished room with a dirt floor. She failed to respond to medical treatment and steadily declined both physically and mentally. She ate lice, bit her dustclothes to pieces, babbled incoherently, and was generally irritating and embarrassing to the whole family. One servant even suggested that she be given poison to end her life. As she lingered on, she cast a pall over the whole compound; and when news of her death reached the family at dinner one evening, everyone, except Pa Chin and his mother, heaved a sigh of relief. Having neither kin nor friends, Yang Sao was hastily buried in an unmarked grave. A month or so later, Pa Chin learned from his mother that Yang Sao had been a widow and had served the family for years. Her tragedy was Pa Chin's first encounter with death.

Outside the Li family, changes were taking place quickly. In April 1911 the Manchu government's plan to nationalize all railways met stiff opposition from the business communities in Hunan, Kwangtung, and Hupeh provinces. There were student strikes, business boycotts, and riots. In Szechwan province, opposition to the plan was especially fierce. At one demonstration, the government arrested more than ten petitioners, and when more demonstrators protested, troops opened fire, killing forty-odd people. The government's action led to increasing outcries against its policies and accelerated the revolutionary movement led by Dr. Sun Yat-sen (1866–1925). On October 10, 1911, the revolution began in earnest in Wuchang, Hupeh province. Other provinces rapidly declared their independence from the Manchu government. With the abdication of the Manchu emperor on February 12, 1912, the Republic of China was established. Having anticipated the coming social and political storm, Pa Chin's father had resigned from his post as magistrate of Kuang-yüan early in 1911 and moved his family back to Chengtu.

Leaving the carefree days of Kuang-yüan behind, Pa Chin lived like other affluent seven-year-olds in his grandfather's compound in Chengtu, totally unaware of the political changes taking place. Toward the end of 1911, on the eighteenth day of the eleventh moon by the lunar calendar, rumors circulated that several banks and pawnshops had been looted by rampaging soldiers and the poor. The news brought instant confusion and panic to the family. Treasures were hidden, women and children were evacuated to relatives' homes in different parts of the city, and Pa Chin's father and menservants stood guard over the compound. The looters arrived in early morning but agreed to accept a token payment in cash from the family, having been awed by the muscular and well-armed security force.

News soon came that Dr. Sun Yat-sen's revolutionary army had executed the provincial governor of Szechwan, and that by government decree the queues of both the young and old must be cut off. When two obstinate servants refused to comply with the new law, their queues were cut off for them by the police. Various family members reacted differently to the collapse of the Manchu regime. Pa Chin's grandfather expressed some sentimental sorrow; his father had no comment; his second uncle was sorry that he had lost the rank of a fourth-class official; and his third uncle mockingly styled himself "the poet of a lost country" and proceeded to write poetry under that new appellation. Pa Chin himself was too young to have any meaningful opinions.[5]

Besides playing with his cousins and studying with a tutor, Pa Chin spent a lot of time with the servants, sometimes assisting them with their work. He vividly remembered that one opium-addicted servant was dismissed from work and later died a penniless beggar, that another servant hanged himself after leaving the family, and how deeply attached he was to a sedan-chair carrier named Chou.

Thin and feeble, lying by his pipe in the stable, Chou had no living kin, his wife having run away with his best friend and his son having died in a war. But his spirit was intact and he would tell and retell his life's story to Pa Chin, and he taught the youth the importance of being true to oneself: "Be a good man, be honest in dealing with others, and never take advantage of them regardless of how they treat you." Thoroughly impressed by Chou, Pa Chin considered him one of his three childhood teachers.[6]

This close and warm contact with the servants continued all the time Pa Chin was growing up, liberating him from his elders' rigid prejudices and making him appreciative of the virtues of the poor. Having been impressed by generous hearts among the poor and downtrodden during his childhood, he later became their passionate defender.

In the summer of 1914, Pa Chin's mother died after a three-week illness. The full significance of her death was not fully understood amidst the funeral preparations. If Pa Chin had been able to venture forth and then withdraw into his mother's protective understanding, that time had now passed. Once the funeral was over, he felt a loss which could not be replaced by his new stepmother's love. Four months later, another tragedy struck. His eldest sister died.

His mother's death left a permanent scar on his psyche. In novel after novel, his fictional characters seem unable to shake off the memories of their mothers, probably a reflection of Pa Chin's psychological dependence on his. Even as late as 1929 he included these words in a sentimental essay entitled "Wo ti hsin" ("My Heart"): "In this wide ocean of blood and tears, what does one person's heart amount to? What can it do? Mother, . . . please take away my heart. I don't need it anymore. But my mother has been dead for many years."[7]

In 1917 his father died. The loss of both parents within three years was a hard blow. In *Yi* (*Memoirs*) he wrote: "The first blow in my life was my mother's death; then came my father's. At that time I was very young and I should have been a child sheltered and protected by my parents. One blow after another was too much for me to bear."[8] His father's death symbolically ended his childhood innocence and opened his eyes to the hatred and perfidy within his family, which had been well hidden by its facade of family togetherness and harmony.

II *Political Awareness*

Late in 1917 Pa Chin's grandfather allowed the boy to attend English classes at a YMCA school in the belief that a knowledge of English would help Pa Chin obtain a well-paying position in the postal service. However, during that one month at school, Pa Chin was sick three times. Therefore, his grandfather insisted he continue by taking private lessons at home. Ever since his father's death, his grandfather had been kind to him. Gradually he began to see his grandfather less as a stereotyped figure and more as a person.

In 1915 Ch'en Tu-hsiu (1879–1942) founded a magazine called *Ch'ing-nien* (*Youth*), later renamed *Hsin Ch'ing-nien* (*New Youth*). Ch'en advocated the abolition and repudiation of obsolete institutions and values and the adoption of new ideas. In 1916, Ch'en was the dean of the School of Letters at National Peking University, then under the leadership of President Ts'ai Yuan-p'ei. National Peking University had a distinguished faculty and was the hub of much intellectual activity, reflecting the full spectrum of ideas from the most conservative to the most radical. In 1917 and 1918 *New Youth* and other progressive magazines mushroomed, all advocating a critical examination of the old China and the adoption of Western ideas.

These intellectual activities in Peking reached a peak in 1919 in the May Fourth Incident, leading to what was later known as the May Fourth Movement. The incident occurred when it became known that England, France, and Italy had secretly agreed to Japan's claim to the privileges previously granted Germany in Shantung province and that the warlord government in Peking had unconditionally acquiesced. On May 4, 1919, more than three thousand students demonstrated in Peking against both the foreign powers and the unpatriotic Chinese officials who had sold out China's interests. At first, the demonstration was peaceful; but after the police arrested thirty-two demonstrators, the students reacted violently. They soon garnered support from many parts of the country and started a national outcry of indignation. The results were the release of those arrested, the resignation of the pro-Japanese officials, and the refusal of the Chinese representatives to sign the Treaty of Versailles.[9] The May Fourth Incident convinced intellectuals of the need to espouse new ideas to educate the people to oppose imperialism and to direct their literary activities so as to hclp build a ncw China. Within six months some four hundred new periodicals, written in the vernacular, appeared on the market.[10]

Meanwhile, in Chengtu, Pa Chin and his brothers avidly read newspapers and periodicals from Shanghai and Peking. Pa Chin recalled:

When the May Fourth Movement erupted, there were frantic reports in the newspapers, and an alarm bell sounded even in our quiet family. Eldest Brother awakened from his wasted youth. At that time I was fourteen-and-a-half years old. With my two brothers I avidly devoured local news reports about the student movements in Peking and in Shanghai. Later the local papers reprinted essays from the *New Youth* and from *Mei-chou p'ing-lun (Weekly Comment)*. These essays deeply stirred us; we felt they said what was in our hearts but did not know how to express.

Then Eldest Brother located the bookstore in town that specialized in selling those publications. He bought a copy of *New Youth* and two or three copies of *Weekly Comment*. We read them intently and happily. Every sentence ignited us, and we were overwhelmed by the new ideas and the emotion-charged words. Later we interested Cousin Hsiang and even Sixth Sister in them also. Sixth Sister subsequently subscribed to another copy of *New Youth*.

New Youth, Hsin ch'ao (New Tide), Weekly Comment, Hsing-ch'i p'ing-lun (Sunday Comment), Shao-nien Chung-kuo (Youth's China), Shao-nien shih-chieh (Youth's World), Pei-ching ta-hsüeh hsüeh-sheng chou-k'an (Weekly Periodical of the Peking University Students) . . . all reached our hands. In Chengtu, there were also *Hsing-ch'i jih (Sunday), Hsüeh-sheng ch'ao (Student Tide), Wei-ke-lieh (Weekly)* and similar periodicals. . . .[11]

At the same time Pa Chin also became interested in Kropotkin's "An Appeal to the Young" (1880), an eloquent exhortation to political activity. Directed specifically to the young, "urging them to put their talents and technical training at the service of the workers and to forego lives of personal gain" and "calculated to fire the idealism of youth," the pamphlet moved Pa Chin deeply.[12] Of the many axioms found in the pamphlet, Pa Chin was amused by this one: "Reading forbidden books on snowy evenings behind closed doors is life's supreme pleasure."[13] Partly influenced by Kropotkin, he became dissatisfied with merely reading and wanted to do something positive.

But no one gave him any guidance. He wrote to Ch'en Tu-hsiu, the editor of *New Youth,* but received no reply. He then obtained a copy of a Chinese translation of Leopold Kampf's *Yeh wei-yang*

(*On the Eve*). It opened his eyes to the tragedy of the youth of another country in their heroic struggle to win liberty and happiness for the people.[14] Then he read works by the anarchist Emma Goldman. Her essays so overwhelmed him that he called her his "spiritual mother" and later corresponded with her. In his reading, Pa Chin was attracted to anarchism's total attack upon those institutions, attitudes, and theoretical positions which were based upon the acceptance of authority, and to its belief in man's reason, goodness, and perfectibility.

His opportunity for action finally came. After reading an article in a local newspaper called *Pan yüeh* (*Semi-monthly*), he wrote to the editor and offered to join its *Shih she* (Equitable Society), an anarchist organization. The editor brought him the reply in person and invited him to a meeting. There he met four other young people whom he considered "full of passion, belief, and dedication." Disclosing his innermost thoughts, his anguish, and his hopes to his new friends, he received from them "friendship, trust, and courage." In his imagination he transformed the small living room where the meeting was held into a "heaven" and compared himself to "a boat having finally found shelter during a storm."[15]

He and his new friends formed a new organization called the *Chün she* (Equity Society). Identifying himself as an anarchist, he and his friends wrote and published articles and books, communicated with other members of the society, recruited new members, and distributed propaganda in the streets. Sometimes imagining themselves in danger of being arrested by government agents, they each took different routes to their meeting places. And when they got there, they would heave sighs of relief. Sharing a common bond of dedication to the anarchist cause and a willingness to sacrifice their personal happiness, they looked forward to a better tomorrow and dreamed that a new world would emerge like the sun rising out of the darkness.[16]

It is not difficult to understand why Pa Chin was attracted to anarchism. Born in 1904, in the disastrous decade between the Boxer Rebellion of 1900 and the establishment of the Republic in 1912, he was aware of the cataclysmic changes engulfing China, the suffering of the peasants, the exploitation of the urban workers, the humiliation of China at the hands of foreign powers, the refusal of the Manchu rulers to accept genuine reforms, the less-than-ideal success of the revolution of 1911, the betrayal of Dr. Sun

Yat-sen's principles by Yüan Shih-k'ai (1859–1916) and the rape of China by corrupt, self-centered warlords.

At home, Pa Chin saw the luxurious life-style of his family, who lived in a spacious compound staffed by more than twenty male and female servants and was maintained primarily by rents from land leased to farmers. He saw too the debased life of the servants who toiled and slaved for his family with little recognition or reward. He resented the social injustice upon which his family depended for its standard of living and was disgusted by the constant bickering among his relatives and by their unproductive lives. He considered his grandfather's control of the family to be authoritarian and called his family a "despotic kingdom" with outdated customs and rules which stifled individual growth and fostered hypocrisy and deception.[17] Moreover, he considered his eldest brother, Li Yao-mei, a prime victim of the traditional Chinese family system. A bright young man, his eldest brother had married a woman of his father's choice, discontinued his studies, and taken charge of the household after the death of his father. Angry at the system and at himself, his eldest brother would take out his frustrations by breaking the glass windows of his sedan-chair late at night. Every time Pa Chin saw his eldest brother commit this wanton act of frustration, his heart writhed in sympathetic anguish.

Like his alleged namesake, Peter Kropotkin, Pa Chin soon turned his talents to writing. Kropotkin edited a journal called *Vremennik* (*Chronicle*), which the Russian anarchist and his brother distributed to a small number of friends;[18] similarly, Pa Chin wrote articles in vernacular Chinese and distributed propaganda pamphlets in the streets of Chengtu, and then edited a publication called *Semi-monthly*. Because of its advocacy of such radical ideas as haircuts for women, a practice contrary to the customs of the time, government censors suspended *Semi-monthly* after its twenty-fourth issue. Pa Chin then joined the editorial board of *Ching ch'ün* (*Warning the People*), a magazine which published only one issue. Six months later he took charge of still another magazine: *P'ing-min chih sheng* (*Voice of the Proletariat*), which published radical articles and waged a continuous battle with government censors.[19]

Among his friends in the *Semi-monthly* office, a colleague named Wu impressed Pa Chin the most. Wu had voluntarily left the foreign-language institute to become a tailor's apprentice in order to practice his personal belief that only those who work should eat. He worked in the tailor's shop daily until late in the afternoon and then went to work at *Semi-monthly*. Despite fingers full of punctures caused by his nearsightedness, he never complained about the hardships of life and supported the magazine with all his resources. To raise money for it, he even pawned his cotton-padded gown. As a man whose deeds matched his words, he taught Pa Chin the need for courage and perseverance in carrying out one's beliefs.[20]

On Chinese New Year's Eve in 1919, Pa Chin's grandfather died. Pa Chin recalled that occasion as follows:

During the New Year period, other families were filled with joy, with strings of firecrackers exploding from one house to the next. But amidst the joy in other families, we prostrated before the family altar, mourning Grandfather's demise.

Our grief was partially hypocritical, because not much more than a week after Grandfather's death, his sons were sitting in his very own room busily dividing up his property and quarreling amongst themselves in front of Grandfather's memorial picture.

But unfortunately, Grandfather knew nothing of these goings-on, or he would have been disappointed with his dream of "five generations living under one roof." I think his hysteria during his last days was not entirely without cause.

Grandfather was an able man. After his father's death he served as a magistrate for many years before "retiring to the countryside." He had bought a lot of land and property, built a handsome compound, collected antiques and scrolls, married twice, acquired two concubines, fathered five sons and one daughter, and even saw a great-grandson. Yet he had also made his sons into mutual enemies and sown the seeds of permanent family discord. And he himself could not escape the fate of dying in loneliness. No one truly loved him; no one really understood him.[21]

After his grandfather's death, Pa Chin's third uncle ruled the family. Pa Chin felt that the family had gone from bad to worse, but, in fact, he had more freedom to do as he pleased.

In the summer of 1920, his elder brother, Li Yao-lin, and he attended a foreign language institute in Chengtu. He studied there for two and a half years but did not receive a diploma because he did not have the necessary middle-school credentials. His treatment by this institute prompted his stepmother and his eldest brother to send him and his elder brother to study in Shanghai.

In the spring of 1923 he and this brother left Chengtu. His eldest brother sorrowfully bade them good-bye at the pier; Pa Chin, too, was stricken with sadness in leaving behind his eldest brother and the others whom he loved to be victimized by the family system.[22] Despite his sadness, he confidently envisioned his future as bright and promising. Having been exposed to many new ideas, and having participated in social activities and edited magazines, he felt he had had considerable social experience. Moreover, he said he had learned love from his mother, faith in himself from the sedan-chair carrier Chou, and self-sacrifice from Wu.[23] His motto at the time was "Struggle is life. Life is progress."[24]

III   *Literary Career*

Near the end of spring in 1923, Pa Chin and his elder brother arrived in Shanghai. Six months later, they went to Nanking to attend a middle school affiliated with Tung-nan University. Without friends or relatives to look after them, the two read, day-dreamed, and waited for letters from their eldest brother. After graduating from middle school in Nanking in 1925, Pa Chin left his brother, who later became a teacher, and went back to Shanghai. He intended to take the entrance examination for the National Peking University, but illness and the May Thirtieth Incident derailed his plan.

The May Thirtieth Incident stemmed from labor problems. At the time there were many foreign-owned plants in Shanghai, no less than twenty-seven of them owned by Japanese. The wages paid to the Chinese workers were low and their treatment harsh. On May 15, a fracas broke out between Chinese workers and Japanese supervisory personnel at one Japanese-owned factory. The Japanese opened fire on the Chinese workers, killing one and seriously wounding several others. On May 30, there was a massive demonstration of several thousand people in Nanking Road and the foreign-controlled police of the International Settlement opened fire, killing ten demonstrators and wounding fifty. On May 31, the Chinese organized a general strike which paralyzed the city; as a protest against the Nanking Road massacre, many Chinese throughout the country held sympathetic strikes.[25]

Pa Chin was in Shanghai at the time. Sympathetic to the workers, he later used what he observed at the time as the basis of his novel *Ssu-ch'ü ti t'ai-yang* (*The Setting Sun*), which sought the betterment of workers' welfare and stressed hatred of foreign interests.

On January 15, 1927, Pa Chin left Shanghai for Marseilles aboard a French mailboat, the *Angers*. He later described his sentimental feelings on that day:

When I stepped onto the deck of the boat, I bade a temporary farewell to my native Chinese soil. With a grieving heart I stood on the deck watching the boat slowly pulling away from the shore and I did not turn around until the tall buildings along the Whampoa River and the foreign warships were completely out of sight. With tears welling up in my eyes, I whispered softly: "Good-bye, my unfortunate country."[26]

The mailboat stopped at Hong Kong, Saigon, Singapore, Columbo, Jibuti on the Red Sea, and Port Said before arriving in Marseilles.

Marseilles impressed Pa Chin with its broad, clean streets and its tall buildings. During a brief layover, he purchased a copy of Zola's short stories. From Marseilles he went to Paris, where he rented a small, poorly ventilated room on the fifth floor of a dilapidated hotel. His life was cheerless. Occasionally, his few friends visited him. Most of the time, he stayed in his room and read, walked in the nearby Jardin du Luxembourg and studied French at a night school sponsored by the Alliance Française. After his evening classes, he sometimes walked to a nearby cemetery to touch the gravestone of Rousseau, whom Tolstoy had hailed as "the world's conscience in the eighteenth century."[27]

Reading and boredom gnawed away at his youth. His only diversions, he claimed, were the rumblings of heavy trucks passing through his street and watching customers coming in and out of a corner café. Homesick, he longed for news of his brothers and friends and read with horror of the political developments in Shanghai, including the purge of Communists by Chiang Kai-shek. To combat loneliness he began to write the novel *Mieh-wang* (*Destruction*) and to translate Kropotkin's *Ethics, Origins and Developments* into Chinese. Better to prepare himself for works of translation, he read Plato, Aristotle, and the Bible.[28]

Boarding at a high school in Château-Thierry on the Marne in the summer of 1928, Pa Chin found life more pleasant and deeply appreciated the company of two other Chinese students who boarded at the same school. The trio took short walks after breakfast every morning and longer walks in the evening, freely discussing subjects of common interest. But soon the two Chinese students left, leaving Pa Chin once again to the solitary pursuit of reading and writing. He familiarized himself with the literature related to the French and Russian revolutions, the trial of the Chicago anarchists of 1886, and with other radical literature. During this period he also acquired the pen name "Pa Chin," presumably reflecting the influence of Bakunin and Kropotkin.[29] Many of his writings at the time were on Russian populism and on the French revolutionary movements.

After two years in France, he returned to China in 1928, without a diploma or a degree. Later he wrote: "I learned nothing, not even French. I just read a bunch of books haphazardly, and wrote a novel called *Destruction*."[30] In fact, he had become a writer. Since the writing profession was held in low esteem by the Chinese, he was a disappointment to his eldest brother and even to himself. His eldest brother had wanted him to become an engineer, a profession which would bring honor to their ancestors, and he himself had wanted to study economics. What he had acquired instead was an extensive knowledge of radical literature.

China in 1928 was as chaotic as it had been in late 1926. Chiang Kai-shek's Northern Expedition did not achieve its objectives. Warlords controlled more of China than did Chiang's Nanking government. While Chiang controlled Nanking, Shanghai, the provinces of Chekiang, Anhwei, Kiangsu, and Kiangsi, such warlords as Feng Yü-hsiang (1882–1948) controlled the rest of China.[31] Meanwhile in Shanghai, labor unrest continued; in 1928 alone there had been one hundred and forty strikes there. In the countryside, peasants continued to suffer at the hands of landlords and from the whims of capricious nature.

Under such circumstances, Lu Hsün (1881–1936), China's best-known and most respected writer and critic, rallied young men and women to the use of writing as a weapon to effect social change. After the serial publication of *Destruction* in *Hsiao-shuo yüeh-pao* (*Fiction Monthly*) from January through April, 1929, Pa Chin responded to Lu Hsün's call, intending to use his writing to express his personal views and to propagate anarchist ideas.

In the same year, his eldest brother came to Shanghai. Unselfishly, he had helped Pa Chin study in Shanghai and later in France. Having been separated for six years, the two brothers were delighted to be reunited. They chatted about family affairs and visited Shanghai's scenic areas. After a month, the brother

returned to Chengtu. The parting was sad for both; Pa Chin
described it as follows:

...I saw him off at his ship. Tears could be seen on his face. I shook his
hand and managed to say: "Take care." As I was about to leave, he told
me to wait. He entered his cabin and took a record out of his suitcase and
said, sobbing: "Take this and listen to it." It was "Sonny Boy" by Gracie
Fields, which I had purchased for him from a foreign firm only two weeks
earlier. He knew I liked it and he wanted me to have it; but I knew he liked
it, too. At first I was reluctant to take it, especially since he liked it very
much. But then I realized that I had disobeyed him many times over the
years and should not unnecessarily make him unhappy.... I took it from
him silently; words cannot describe how I felt.³²

In the spring of 1931, following unwise business ventures and
financial reverses, the eldest brother committed suicide. It was a
shock to Pa Chin, despite the fact that he had received ominous
letters from him. He never believed that his brother would take his
life, and in a long and moving essay entitled "Ta Ko" ("Eldest
Brother"), he wrote: "I only know he did not want to die, and he
did not have to die. I know he wrote and destroyed his 'last words'
at least three times. Even in the fourth version, he unconsciously
cried out 'I don't want to die.' Yet, like an honest gentleman, he
'ate his own fruit.' As a result, among many hypocritical gentlemen
he lost face and left a life of suffering to his wife, a son, and four
daughters."³³ After the suicide, debtors, including uncles and
aunts, were unwilling to forgive his eldest brother's debts and
pressed the widow for payment. Considering his brother a typical
and representative victim of the archaic Chinese family system, Pa
Chin attacked that system vehemently in his *Chi-liu* (*Turbulent
Stream*) trilogy.

Previously, in 1930, Pa Chin had completed *The Setting Sun* and
a volume of short stories called *Fu-ch'ou* (*Revenge*). Driven by an
internal fire, he wrote ceaselessly. Under intense personal anguish,
he completed *Chia* (*Family*), the first in his *Turbulent Stream*
trilogy; *Hsin-sheng* (*New Life*); *Wu* (*Fog*); and a volume of short
stories called *Kuang-ming* (*Light*). In the winter of 1931 he spent a
week in a coal mine, the experience of which became the basis for a
novelette originally called *Meng-ya* (*Germs*) but later retitled *Hsüeh*
(*Snow*) and published in 1934.³⁴

In 1931, Japanese forces shelled Chapei, a suburb of Shanghai,
and on January 28, 1932, Shanghai itself. Chapei had been Pa

Chin's home since his return from France, but fortunately, during the bombing attack, he was aboard a train to Nanking. After a few anxious days in Nanking, he returned to Shanghai. Everywhere he saw low-flying Japanese warplanes and scenes of destruction, and was unable to return to his Chapei home. On March 2, 1932, Chapei fell under Japanese control, and his *New Life* manuscript, completed in August 1931, was destroyed in a fire that engulfed his printer's shop. Staying with a friend, outraged by Japan's war of aggression, he wrote *Hai ti meng (Dream on the Sea)*, a propagandistic piece indicting the Japanese invaders.

Several times he tried to return to his home in Chapei to retrieve his belongings. Once, accompanied by a friend, he entered Chapei only to see "charred broken logs and roof tiles; streets bombed beyond recognition; everywhere debris and empty house frames...." And in the corner of a collapsed wall they saw several charred bodies, so shriveled that they no longer resembled human remains. Japanese soldiers eventually stopped them and one, speaking the Shanghai dialect, told them to proceed no further.[35]

Several days later, Pa Chin and another friend entered Chapei through Hu Chiang Road, a street so cluttered with mounds of debris that he could not recognize it. At a crossroads he saw proud Japanese soldiers standing on piles of sandbags; after they were questioned by the Japanese, he and his friend were allowed to enter the restricted area. With considerable difficulty he located his house and happily retrieved a few undestroyed books from among the ruined furniture. Emotionally distraught, in his mind's eye he saw such scenes as a penniless couple returning to their home province, his own interrogation by the Japanese, the gruesome sight of human limbs being devoured by stray dogs, and acts of violence committed by Japanese soldiers against Chinese.

In 1932 he wrote *Ch'un-t'ien li ti ch'iu-t'ien (Autumn in Spring)*, a romantic tale, and *Sha-ting (The Antimony Miners)*, a proletarian novelette.[36] In the spring of 1932, Pa Chin's elder brother, Li Yao-lin, came from Tientsin to see him. They visited the famed West Lake in Hangchow and other places before Yao-lin took a train from Nanking to return to Tientsin. Again, the parting was painful. Even though there were frequent Japanese bombing attacks on Tientsin, Pa Chin could not dissuade his brother from returning there. In an essay called "Wo ti hu-hao" ("My Cries"), Pa Chin expressed his appreciation that his brother had made so many financial sacrifices for their eldest brother's family, and his own frustrations as a writer. He spoke of his anguish at being slandered by other writers and questioned whether he should continue his writing career.[37]

Pa Chin spent the summer of 1933 in Hong Kong and Canton. Unlike the war-ravaged north, the south was unscathed by the war and remained prosperous. The streets in Hong Kong were thronged with men in white suits and hats and young women in short-sleeved blouses and long pants. The view of the "Fragrant Harbor" from Victoria Peak was exquisite; and swimming at Repulse Bay beach was pleasant.

Shortly afterwards, he went by boat to Canton. His friends arranged for him to attend a meeting between peasants and landlords; he saw the auctioning off of a pathetic sixteen-year-old girl at a dinner party; elderly men keeping young prostitutes; and the proliferation of gambling and opium dens along the Pearl River. All this confirmed his belief that Canton was a city teeming with social problems which were temporarily hidden by peace and prosperity.

In July 1933 Pa Chin returned to Shanghai; in September he left for Tientsin. On the train to Tientsin, he noted: "As a man journeys north, he keenly feels that he ages by the minute, particularly if he has just returned from the south and is used to southern villages, southern cuisine, and southern air. The green banyan trees of the south are no longer visible. Steeped in tradition, everything in the north has a feeling of heaviness."[38] On the train, he admired the attractiveness of the wide plains and associated the bare mountains and the lack of greenery with the northerners' stoic ruggedness. From Tientsin he went to Peking, where he contributed articles to and served on the editorial board of *Wen-hsüeh chi-k'an* (*Literature Quarterly*).

He worked compulsively day and night but had doubts about the effectiveness of his work as a weapon which would effect social change.[39] In 1933 he declared that his writing had little impact on the masses and only wasted his energy and life;[40] in a short story called "Kuang-ming" ("Light") a writer, presumably Pa Chin himself, wonders aloud: "Writing books — what's the use? It can only bring sorrow to mankind."[41] Frequently, in a mood of self-pity, he said that his work had "extracted" too much of his flesh and blood.[42] But in calmer moments, he acknowledged that he did achieve "satisfaction" from his writing and considered his work therapeutic for his mental health.[43]

Despite his widespread fame as a writer, Pa Chin continued to be harassed by government censors who considered many of his works subversive. Resenting the stifling political climate in China and seeking greater freedom and a better perspective on life, he went to Japan and stayed there from November 1934 through July 1935. His Japanese sojourn was disappointing. In his essay "Fan-hsing" ("Galaxy of Stars"), written in January 1935, a fictional character presumably speaking for Pa Chin, asks: "Why did I come here [to Japan]? The freedom I craved is nonexistent here. I have left a 'crooked road' for a little temporary peace and quiet in a strange land and spent my time on useless books. Isn't this a life of indulgence?"[44] Like his fictional character, Pa Chin experienced even greater political oppression in Japan than he had in China. Because of the impending visit of Henry P'u Yi, the Emperor of Manchukuo, to Tokyo, Pa Chin was arrested by the Japanese police and detained for a day in a police station, an experience which later became the basis of his short story "Jen" ("Man"). In short, during his most productive period, Pa Chin was deeply disturbed by inner discord and a search for his true self. He was haunted by his call for action by others, while he himself remained inactive, and by his gradual awareness of his own inability to change things.

In a less than happy mood, Pa Chin returned to China in July 1935 to become the editor of the Wen-hua sheng-huo (Culture and Life) Publishing Company in Shanghai. He edited and published many Chinese and foreign classics as well as works by young Chinese writers. He also translated a number of Turgenev's works from Russian into Chinese and wrote *Ch'un* (*Spring*) and *Ch'iu* (*Autumn*), sequels to the novel *Family*. Among his prose works of the period were *K'ung-su* (*J'Accuse*), *Yi* (*Memoirs*), *Tien-ti* (*Drops*), and *Tuan-chien* (*Short Notes*).

On October 19, 1936, Lu Hsün died in Shanghai. Pa Chin was one of the pallbearers and later wrote a moving memorial hailing Lu Hsün as a man who loved the young, who was a pioneer fighter in man's liberation movement, and who held up the torch of thought to guide millions of the young toward the light.[45]

IV *The War Years*

After the outbreak of the Sino-Japanese War in 1937, Pa Chin wrote war poems, essays, and letters to condemn the wanton Japanese bombings and to praise the heroic efforts of the Chinese.[46] When the Chinese troops withdrew from Shanghai following a valiant defense of the city, Pa Chin moved to the French Concession, an area still controlled by the French. In sorrow, he heard of the fall of Nanking (December 13, 1937) and of the atrocities committed there by the Japanese, and of the fall of other major Chinese cities including Tsingtao and Hangchow.

In 1937 and 1938, besides his work at the Culture and Life Publishing Company, he served on the editorial boards of *Feng-huo* (*Beacon*) and *Na-han* (*Outcry*) magazines and resumed his writing of *Spring*. In April 1938, after he saw the galley proofs of *Spring,* he left Shanghai once again.

In Canton he wrote the first volume of his *Huo* (*Fire*) trilogy and prepared *Meng yü tsui* (*Dream and Inebriation*), a volume of essays, for publication. In contrast to his last visit, the city now suffered under constant Japanese bombings. During one raid, six Japanese warplanes dropped bombs near his office as he sat in his rattan chair and buried his head in the proof sheets on his desk. After the raid, his desk was covered by a layer of dust and his colleagues looked very much shaken.

Later he visited a bombed-out area with a friend and saw the totality of destruction: buildings collapsed and streets covered with rubble, loose electric wires and downed electricity poles. One eyewitness told him that a bomb had fallen near a French church, that more than twenty truckloads of wounded had been sent to the Chung-san Hospital, and that he had seen a man running about with his severed arm and a woman, half of whose face had been torn away, holding a headless infant in her arms.[47]

The war cured Pa Chin's fits of depression. Fired by patriotism, he described the wartime Canton to a friend as follows: "This place is probably different from yours. Here there is neither courage nor cowardice. The residents do not love to die, but they are not afraid to die either. They treat death as a common event. If it visits them, they allow it to come into their houses without any fuss from the neighbors. One man dies, others continue to work. One house is destroyed, others continue to be inhabited. As soon as the blood on the balcony is washed away, the living walk on it again. Man falls, man bleeds — these are common sights. Even severed heads and limbs are not considered tragic. The dead are buried, the living continue to do their jobs — only working harder...."[48]

Soon Pa Chin was on the road. In September 1938, via boat, bus, and train, he went to Changsha and from there to Wuhan. He noted that the overcrowded trains, buses, and boats were favorite bombing targets and that people invariably became hysterical during bombing attacks. In Wuhan he wanted to see for himself the Chinese preparations to hold back the Japanese, who were already nearby. Life appeared normal; he visited friends and held discussions with them in his hotel room. Though he had to sleep in a bed that was too short, nevertheless he felt his stay in Wuhan to be exhilarating.

Early in October, Pa Chin returned to Canton, a city now besieged by the Japanese. One night while in the famous Columbus Café, which was situated on the second floor of a multi-storied building, he and several friends watched thousands of marching young men demonstrating their determination to defend the city; and everywhere he heard discussions of defense plans. But only a few days later, he noted that the fashionable ladies who regularly patronized the café had left and been replaced by men in uniform. One man told him that he was a music professor at the local Sun Yat-sen University but felt obligated to join the others in defending the city. However, with the massive exodus of people from the city, its usual calm was soon replaced by panic; and with the departure of the printers, his work in Canton came to a virtual halt.

On October 20, 1938, Pa Chin went by boat to Wuchow, Kwangsi province. While in Wuchow, he heard the disappointing news that the Chinese troops had evacuated Wuhan, news which effectively demolished the earlier and widely held belief that the Chinese would defend Wuhan at all costs. From Wuchow he went to Kweilin, another city frequently bombed by the Japanese. In Kweilin, he edited the magazine *Wen-ts'un tsa-chih* (*Literary Miscellany*), but he had to spend most of his time in air-raid shelters.

Returning to Shanghai in 1939, he lived in the French Concession, where he was joined by his elder brother, who had left Tientsin. In addition to supervising his brother's translations from the Russian, he translated more of Kropotkin's works and worked on his novel *Autumn*. After the French surrender to Germany in July 1940, he left Shanghai and went to Kunming. He completed the *Fire* trilogy there and then went to Chungking and to Chengtu, his hometown.

In 1941 he returned to Kweilin and lived there for the next three years with many side trips to Kweiyang, Kunming, Chungking, and Chengtu.

On May 8, 1944, he married Miss Ch'en Yun-chen in Kweiyang. She had been a student in the Foreign Languages Department of the National Southwest Associated Universtiy in Kunming, and he wanted her to return to Kunming to finish her studies, but she insisted on accompanying him to Kweilin. In May and June of 1944, the war situation deteriorated still further. Pressed by the final Japanese attack, the Chinese army retreated in Hunan and Kwangsi, and on June 18, Changsha fell to the Japanese.

As a result, Pa Chin and his wife moved to Chungking, the provisional capital of the Nationalist government. There they stayed until the war ended in 1945. Poor, they had to live in one small room, and saw many of their friends die of the rampaging tuberculosis. Pa Chin wrote a series of obituaries, collectively entitled *Huai-nien* (*Reminiscences*). In its preface, he characterized his deceased friends as ordinary people who "never did anything to harm others. They never cheated, they were humble and congenial, and responsibly did their work; they were poor, but they had rich hearts, and were sincere toward others...."[49] In addition, he wrote three major works: *Ti-ssu ping-shih* (*Ward Number Four*), *Ch'i-yüan* (*Leisure Garden*), and *Han-yeh* (*Cold Nights*).

The Japanese surrendered in August 1945. But the victory did not bring much joy to Pa Chin. His feelings toward the victory were vividly expressed in his novel *Cold Nights* and in his dramatized essay "Wu t'i" ("No Title"), written in 1946. Part of the essay describes Chungking one and a half months after the Japanese surrender:

...It was reported that repairs were still being made, and therefore there was no electricity in the city. It rained in the afternoon and turned cold in the evening. Walking on the slightly wet pavement, I went to visit a friend. The sky was dark, and the stores' acetylene lamps on both sides of the street were so dim that they did not light up the street itself. There were but few pedestrians, and my thin clothing was unable to protect me from the chill which made me shiver once or twice. "Autumn is truly here," I said softly....

I stood on a street corner, suddenly remembering that it was the same place where the people had hysterically celebrated the victory for more than a day. A huge crowd had gathered and people were laughing, screaming, jumping, and clowning with one another. Little children were chasing after jeeps, and adults raised their fists in happiness. I too shared their joy. But today, in the darkness, I could find no trace of that laughter. Where had all those people and their laughter gone?

"Sir, we are refugees from Kweilin," said an elderly woman-beggar emerging from the dark and stretching out her thin hand.

I put my hand into the pocket of my long gown but found nothing to give her. I sadly shook my head and said no.
. . .

The smell of acetylene lamps reached my nostrils.
"When are you leaving for your home?" I overheard one man ask another.
"I can't leave. Steamer tickets are not for ordinary folks."
"Try to find some way. Be a stowaway."
"One of my relatives became a stowaway and was arrested."
"Your situation is not too bad. Even if you can't leave Szechwan, you can afford to spend a few months here. If I couldn't leave, I'd starve by next month at the latest. Who would have thought that this is what victory would amount to?"[50]

Like the characters in this dramatized essay, Pa Chin, too, was eager to leave Chungking; he returned to Shanghai two months later. His elder brother had been seriously ill and died in December 1945. In a moving memorial essay, Pa Chin recalled their student days in Nanking in 1925: "During those days we had no recreation, no social activities, and no friends, except for three or four school-mates who lived in our boardinghouse. Every morning we went to school and every afternoon we came home together. When it rained, we shared one umbrella with the rain soaking through our blue gowns. In the summer we slept on netless wooden beds, without any protection from the mosquitoes. Our frequent dreams were the only diversion in our lonely existence."[51] He also recalled how his older brother had unselfishly supported their eldest brother's family on a teacher's salary:

When Eldest Brother suddenly committed suicide, he left a family behind. His family needed us. You took it upon yourself to send money to them every month. Your small income became even more limited and your own plans dissipated like cloud castles in the sky. A heavy millstone was tied around your slightly raised head which you would never be able to lift high again. Like a bird with a broken wing, you lost forever the hope of soaring in the air.
You quietly took it all. . . . You lived in the staff quarters for Nankai teachers for ten years. . . . Going to the movies was your only recreation. . . . I had gone to Tientsin to see you three times, but the last time I went I could only spend one night with you. I could see your weariness, your loneliness, your "autumnness." I tried to talk to you about yourself but you wouldn't let me. Sometimes I pressed you, but to shut off my

questioning you'd always say: "What else is there to do?" You always had a smile, but it was a lonely and weary one.[52]

In addition to being troubled by his brother's death, he was also very much disenchanted with the postwar Nationalist government. In 1946 his output was limited to a few memorial essays in memory of departed friends. He resumed his post as editor for the Culture and Life Publishing Company in Shanghai, and began to translate Kropotkin's *Speeches of a Rebel*. He continued to support anarchist activities in China and kept up his connections with anarchists abroad; he also showed a greater interest in Christianity and often met with Father Monsterleet, a Belgian Jesuit who was then writing a book about him. In 1947 he published *Cold Nights* and several short stories.

V *After the Communist Victory*

After the Communist victory in 1949, many writers gravitated to Peking or to Shanghai, where Pa Chin had remained. He was made a vice-chairman of the National Committee of the All-China Federation of Literary and Art Circles and of the All-China Writers' Association, a deputy from Szechwan province to the National People's Congress, and a delegate to several international literary and political congresses. In March 1952 he led a group from the All-China Federation of Literary and Art Circles to Korea and spent seven months there; in August 1953, after the Armistice, he returned to Korea, this time by himself. In 1961 he attended the Emergency Meeting of the Afro-Asian Writers' Conference in Japan, and in 1962 he participated in the Eighth Conference on the Banning of Nuclear Weapons, also in Japan. In 1963 he visited North Vietnam. In addition, he traveled extensively within China and made a much-publicized visit to a steel worker named Chiu Tsai-kung, who had been seriously burned while trying to protect public property.[53]

Due to the Communist party's rigid control over literature, beginning with the expanded party-directed mass-criticism campaign in 1952 and followed by even more stringent controls over literature in 1954–55, few writers before the Communist victory produced much. Ts'ao Yü (1910–), Hsia Yen (1900–), Yeh Sheng-t'ao (1894–), Hsieh Ping-hsin (1903–), Mao Tun (1896–) all quieted their revolutionary fires of the 1930s and early

1940s. Pa Chin wrote cautiously. His visits to Korea led to his writing about the Chinese who fought there in *Ying-hsiung ti ku-shih* (*Stories of Heroes*), which was published in 1953; some of these stories were later translated into English and published by the Foreign Languages Press of Peking under the title *Living Amongst Heroes.*

During the "cheng-feng" or "rectification of working style" campaigns in 1954 and 1955, many old writers were singled out for attack.[54] A young, obscure writer, with the full backing of the party, would single out certain literary works for criticism, and his targets would be expected to confess their ideological inadequacies prior to the Communist victory in 1949. Those who refused would be subjected to harsh punishment. The campaign led to the silencing of Hu Feng (1903–   ) in 1955. Hu had been an influential left-wing writer since the 1930s and had always been faithful to and vocal about Communist causes.

Then the "Hundred Flowers Bloom" campaign began in 1956. In theory, at least, the government invited writers to express their feelings on all subjects. At first reticent, the innocent writers soon expressed their frustrations with the party bureaucracy, corruption on all levels, 'socialist realism,' and other evils. After precisely one year, the government showed it had reversed its policy by attacking Ting Ling (c. 1902–   ), a loyal party member. She was denounced as a "poisonous weed" because of her insistence that writers should be given scope for the expression of their own individuality.

Throughout all these campaigns, Pa Chin had been prudent. For example, during the "Great Leap Forward" movement of 1958, he promised to produce "one long novel, three medium novels and several translations in the course of a year."[55] But in April 1958 he slipped up in a routine article he wrote for *Wen-i pao,* attacking Howard Fast, the American writer who had recently broken with communism. In his article, Pa Chin showed more sympathy with and regret for Fast than was considered proper. Consequently, he was singled out for attack, particularly for his pre-1949 anarchist writings. The campaign against him was fully under way by October 1958, even though he had already publicly apologized for his indiscretion regarding Fast. The campaign against him subsided only after many readers had come to his defense.[56]

Under such circumstances it is understandable why Pa Chin would write, in 1958, that he was totally unsatisfied with the creation of his romantic-anarchist hero in his first novel, *Destruction:*

If Tu Ta-hsin had not had tuberculosis, if he could have had a correct revolutionary path such as communism to follow, he would not have been so lonely. He was waging a futile struggle single-handedly. He would not have "hated all men," including himself. . . . Had there been an organization to direct him, to support him, he would never have felt so lonely and so despairing, or experienced so many internal conflicts, or finally sought death to get rid of his conflicts.[57]

In 1961 Pa Chin confessed that he had lived a life apart from the masses, had fantasized about the world while sitting in his room with a few close friends, and had failed to find a correct path to follow. For instance, in his discussion of the writing of *New Life,* he said:

Our generation of educated youth from capitalist and bourgeois backgrounds was all more or less associated with individualism. I, of course, was no exception. I craved revolution, yet I was unable to renounce individualism; I craved reform, yet I myself never participated in any revolutionary activities; I craved light, yet I was drowned in nostalgic sorrow for those friends who died in darkness. I loudly screamed for progress, yet I was inexorably dragged behind by shadows of the past.[58]

He also admitted his folly in believing that the pen could change society: "Other than a naive and powerless pen, I had no other weapon, and I had not found a correct revolutionary ideology with which to arm myself. I spent whole days writing and never participated in actual struggles. How could I ever inflict any harm on the enemy?"[59] He went on to say that his style was not good because it had too many barbarisms and that because of his translations he had adopted a writing style that resembled foreign sentence patterns. And he maintained that he had benefited greatly from studying the works of other Chinese writers such as Lu Hsun, Yeh Sheng-t'ao, Hsia Mien-tsun (1885–1946), Chu Tzu-ch'ing (1898–1948), and from his old-fashioned private tutors in Chengtu. And lastly, he expressed regret that he had not studied more Chinese classics and learned calligraphy properly.

When he prepared his collected works for publication, he changed the endings of several of them, excising references to anarchism; he denied that he had derived his pen name "Pa Chin" from the first and last syllables of Bakunin's and Kropotkin's names. He also rationalized his acceptance of anarchism as follows:

In the wake of the May Fourth Movement, when I was ready to accept new ideas, I found a brand-new world. I was a little frightened, yet I was overwhelmed by what I read. I tried to absorb everything. Every idea that I could put my hands on, I instantly swallowed. Anything that was new and progressive I loved; anything old and regressive I hated. My mind was simple and I lacked a sense of judgment. What I had read prior to that time were the *Four Books* and the *Five Classics,* and some Chinese and foreign fiction. So I accepted anarchism by reading Kropotkin's little books and other periodicals.... I was never able to give up anarchism. Maybe it was a subconscious way for me to cover up my weakness, my hesitation, and my doubts in order to live a life that was free and yet contradictory, leisurely and yet agonizing.... To tell the truth, I really looked for a leader who could give me guidance, but then I slowly got used to the life the anarchists advocated.[60]

During the Cultural Revolution (1966–1968), regular publications were suspended and old books confiscated or burned. Pa Chin's works were removed from bookstores and libraries and in some cases destroyed. Like other writers of his generation, he was again singled out for attack — for his petit-bourgeois background, his failure to have adopted a more definite revolutionary (read Communist) line in his writing, his lifelong association with anarchists, and even for alleged attacks on the thoughts of Mao Tse-tung (1893–1976). The attacks culminated in an article which appeared on February 26, 1968, in the newspaper *Wen-hui pao* of Shanghai. The article labeled him "the Big Literary Tyrant" and called him other names. A few months later, on June 20, 1968, Red Guards ransacked his home in Shanghai, destroying his art collection and his library, which contained an impressive collection of anarchists literature. Still unsatisfied with their treatment of him, the Red Guards dragged him to the People's Stadium, where he was made to kneel on broken glass and forced to confess his "sins." An eyewitness reported that as insults mounted Pa Chin yelled: "You have your thoughts and I have mine. This is the fact, and you can't change it even if you kill me." Soon afterwards he was put under house arrest.[61]

Since the Cultural Revolution not much has been heard about him; he was believed to be working in Shanghai in 1975. Most recently, in July 1977, he wrote an article for the *Wen-hui pao* in Shanghai revealing his persecution by the Gang of Four.[62]

CHAPTER 2

Early Novels

I Introduction

THE Chinese literati had always accepted the premise that China was the center of the world and that the Chinese were superior to the "barbarians," who looked strange and dressed differently. But this traditional view became obsolete overnight with the defeat of the Chinese by the British during the Opium War of 1839 to 1842. The war marked the beginning of a new awareness of foreigners and foreign powers and of a reevaluation of China and her traditions. It was followed by the T'ai-p'ing Rebellion (1848–65), which signaled the beginning of the end of the Manchu dynasty. The literati became increasingly alarmed at China's rapid decline as revealed by her having to sign so many "unequal treaties" and to cede so many territorial rights to foreign powers. Consequently, the literati sought ways and means to resurrect China, but their efforts got nowhere; the antiforeign agitation culminated in the Boxer Rebellion of 1900, and the granting of even more rights and privileges to the Allied Forces of Japan, Germany, the United States, and five other nations. Even though the Manchu regime was overthrown in 1912 by Dr. Sun Yat-sen and others, China's problems remained and, in fact, became even more serious.

Among these, the most fundamental was the language. Just as China could no longer view herself as the center of the world, classical Chinese, the exclusive language of the scholarly elite, was no longer an adequate national language. In its place, Dr. Hu Shih (1891–1962) urged the adoption of *pai-hua* (vernacular Chinese) in the literary revolution of 1917.

At the same time, Ch'en Tu-hsiu, in his article "On Literary

Revolution," published in *New Youth,* urged the beginning of a new literature which would reflect China's pressing social realities. His call for a new literature earned the support of Lu Hsün, whose brilliant stories "The Diary of a Madman" (1918) and the "True Story of Ah Q" (1921) described the Chinese character in ironic terms. Then, in 1921, the Society for Literary Studies was founded. It advocated "literature for life" and its aim was "literature to improve life." Similarly, the Creation Society, which had been established in 1921, soon changed its aim from the "creation of beauty" to the "destruction of evil."[1]

The call for a new realistic literature became ever more strident during the early 1920s, with China partitioned by warlords and partially controlled by foreigners and with the Chinese largely apathetic to social causes despite their sufferings. In 1926, Kuo Mo-jo (1892-) of the Creation Society wrote a much-discussed essay entitled "Revolution and Literature," which included the following major points:

The demands of the people or of our nation are the same as those of the proletariat in capitalist countries. We demand liberation from economic oppression, mankind's right to exist, equal distribution of goods, a complete eradication of the freedom associated with individualism, and a thoroughly rebellious attitude toward romanticism in literature. . . . Young men! Young men! You must strengthen and enrich your living experience and recognize the major literary trends. You should go among the soldiers, the people, into the factories and participate in the maelstrom of revolution. You must know we demand a literature that is sympathetic to the goals of proletarian socialist realism. Our demands are identical with the masses. . . .[2]

Similarly, in the inaugural edition of the *Creation Monthly* in February 1926, Yü Ta-fu (1894–1945) wrote: "Our ambition is not grandiose. On the less positive side, we just wish to share our powerless sympathy with those warriors who have been bitterly defeated in their struggle for justice. But more positively, we wish to use our feeble voice to promote the reform of the present inequitable social structure."[3]

Writers wrote on social themes and introduced Western literature to the Chinese public. Soon after the turn of the twentieth century, Harriet Beecher Stowe's *Uncle Tom's Cabin* (1852), Upton Sinclair's socialist fiction, the Greek tragedies, the dramas of Ibsen, Shaw, and Eugene O'Neill, the poetry of Walt Whitman, and the works of Goethe were translated into Chinese and warmly received by the public. Various Western theories of literature including the concept of "art for art's sake," the radical idealism of Karl Marx, and the ideas of romanticism, sentimentalism, naturalism, expressionism, and socialist realism were all introduced.[4]

But the main thrust was that art would no longer be relegated to the essentially passive role of portraying or commenting on the conditions of Chinese life; instead, it should become a positive instrument helping to shape ideas, influence behavior, and alter social conditions. Writers should no longer be observers but creative artists. This view gained immediate credence as Chiang Kuang-tz'u (1901–1931), Mao Tun, and Lu Hsün reacted favorably to using such themes as antiimperialism, antifeudalism, and antiwarlordism in literature.

II   *A Writer of Conviction*

Ever since the publication of *Destruction,* Pa Chin has been a popular and prolific writer. He has published more than thirty volumes of novels, novelettes, and short stories, over twenty volumes of travelogues and other prose essays, and more than thirty volumes of translations. Yet he maintained he had never planned to be a writer.

It was entirely by chance that Pa Chin started his writing career. He wrote that when he went to France he wanted to study economics and spend a few years in French classrooms and libraries. Lonely and bored with his life in Paris, he was excited to read about the political activities then taking place in China. Unable to be a part of that political scene, he said he was so agonized that he felt as if a knife were cutting into his heart.[5] Helplessly frustrated, he began to write his first novel, *Destruction,* as a form of self-therapy.

It is not surprising that Pa Chin should have begun as a political writer when one takes his background into consideration. A well-educated young man, he was fully aware of the political and intellectual activities that followed in the wake of the May Fourth Movement, and he must have been quite sympathetic to such goals as "the revelation of human and social realities" advocated by the Society for Literary Studies and the "unrestricted expression of personal feelings" argued by the Creation Society.[6] Moreover, living in Shanghai in 1925, he must also have read Kuo Mo-jo's much-discussed essay "Revolution and Literature" and Yü Ta-fu's essay in the inaugural issue of the *Creation Monthly*. Aware of the trends of the time and influenced by Kropotkin, Lu Hsün, and others, he also viewed literature as an effective means to combat social inequities and to exhort the masses to act. In the preface to his *Tien-yi* (*The Electric Chair*), a volume of short stories, he made clear his literary theory: "What is art after all, if it cannot bring more light to humanity? If it cannot strike a single blow against the demon? . . . No, I want to make a direct appeal to my readers to make them abhor darkness and love light."[7]

Starting with *Destruction* and continuing with *Hsin-sheng* (*New life*) and other political fiction, Pa Chin never wavered in his aim of exposing what he considered to be evil. In *Ai-ch'ing ti san-pu ch'ü* (*The Love Trilogy*), he stressed the importance of having "hsin-yang" (belief), a phrase not clearly defined by him buy implying faith that tomorrow will be made better by the actions of the young:

Passion is not enough. . . . Then there comes belief. Belief does not restrict but strengthens and directs passion. Belief guides passion, facilitates passion to flow smoothly, without being blocked or causing a flood. From *Wu* (*Fog*) to *Yü* (*Rain*), from *Rain* to *Tien* (*Lightning*), belief directs passion comfortably into the sea. . . . The seed planted in *Fog* sprouted in *Rain* and blossomed in *Lightning*. When he read *Lightning,* we see how belief has dominated all and saved all.[8]

Of his *Chi-liu* (*Turbulent Stream*) trilogy Pa Chin wrote:

I've always used my pen as a weapon against the old society and its system [the system before the Communist victory]. If it were not to attack the old inequitable system, I'd never have written fiction. Had I not spent nineteen years living in a big feudal family, had I not personally seen and experienced the many different types of suffering inflicted upon others by the old system, had I not seen many "man-eating-man" tragedies, had I not intensely hated the old system of exploitation and oppression of man by man, had I not been filled with love for the sincere men and women, I'd never have written *Chia* (*Family*), *Ch'un* (*Spring*), and *Ch'iu* (*Autumn*).[9]

And this belief was also apparent in his *Huo* (*Fire*) trilogy. In the postscript to Volume I of *Fire,* he wrote: "In writing this novel I wanted not only to communicate my fervor and indignation but to stimulate other people's courage and strengthen their faith. I also wanted them to see from the activities of these simple youths the hope for a new China."[10]

In short, Pa Chin's theory of literature is similar to what H. G. Wells said about it: "I have never taken any great pains about writing. I am outside the hierarchy of conscious and deliberate writers altogether.... Literature is not jewelry, it has quite other aims than perfection, and the more one thinks of 'how it is done' the less one gets it done...."[11] In other words, Pa Chin and Wells both consider technique to be of secondary importance.

This disregard for technique does not imply that they had no technique. Technique is really what T. S. Eliot means by "convention": "any selection, structure, or distortion, any form or rhythm imposed upon the world of action."[12] In this sense, no writer can say he has no technique or that he eschews technique, for the mere fact that he is a writer means he cannot make such a claim. One can only speak of good and bad, adequate or inadequate technique, but never of the presence or absence of technique.

To evaluate Pa Chin's work properly, one must pay attention to what he says and how he says it. Sometimes his urgent sense of the importance of his material overshadows his use of technical refinements; at other times his use of technique helps him to discover, explore, and develop his subject and to convey its meaning, and results in works replete with meaningful content, with depth and resonance.

Between the years 1927 and 1936 Pa Chin wrote a series of novels: *Mieh-wang* (*Destruction*), *Hsin-sheng* (*New Life*), *Ssu-ch'ü ti t'ai-yang* (*The Setting Sun*), *Chia* (*Family*), *Ch'un-t'ien li ti ch'iu-t'ien* (*Autumn in Spring*), *Hai ti meng* (*Dream on the Sea*), *Sha-ting* (*The Antimony Miners*), *Hsüeh* (*Snow*), *Li-na,* and *Ai-ch'ing ti san-pu ch'ü* (*The Love Trilogy*), consisting of *Wu* (*Fog*), *Yü* (*Rain*), *Tien* (*Lightning*), and an interlude called *Lei* (*Thunder*). Thematically, *Destruction, New Life, Li-na,* and *The Love Trilogy* are stories of revolutionaries; *Family* and *Autumn in Spring* are stories attacking the archaic family system; and *The Setting Sun, Dream on the Sea, The Antimony Miners,* and *Snow* deal with specific social and economic issues.

III   *Revolutionaries*

In discussing the writing of *Destruction,* Pa Chin singled out the influence on him of Bartolomco Vanzetti (1888–1927). In 1927, depressed and lonely, he became interested in the trial of Sacco and Vanzetti in Boston and wrote to Vanzetti, from whom he soon received favorable replies. Vanzetti's encouragement inspired him to complete chapters eleven and thirteen of *Destruction*. Then on August 23, 1927, Sacco and Vanzetti were executed in Boston. Saddened by the news of the execution and by the political campaigns against the Chinese Communists waged by the ruling Kuomintang in 1927, he became aware of what seemed to him to be unjust laws and their enforcement. To him, the Commonwealth of Massachusetts had executed Sacco and Vanzetti on flimsy circumstantial evidence and the Kuomintang had acted without regard for human rights. It was in this frame of mind that he finished writing *Destruction*.

With little idea of what a novel should be, but himself full of grievances, Pa Chin sought to picture an unjust society and preach its destruction. Clumsily, he presents his vision of a corrupt society through the eyes of Tu Ta-hsin (Tu the Big Hearted), who is lonely and tubercular. Tu is shocked to witness an automobile accident in which though a poor man's skull is actually broken open, the driver of the car and his passengers not only receive no punishment but are dealt with politely by the traffic police. With a poet's sensitivity, Tu sees other bizarre happenings: a skinny little boy being beaten by a robust woman and a teenage girl pulling while her grandfather pushes a cart of manure and other incidents. Everywhere Tu seems to hear a voice saying to him: "We were born in poverty, we suffer in poverty, and we shall die in poverty."[13]

Unable to provide more concrete examples of social injustice, Pa Chin shifts his attention to describing Tu's feelings of hatred. For more than a year Tu has been in charge of publicity work for a labor union in Shanghai. His intense hatred of society deprives him of any personal pleasure. He is in love with Miss Li Ching-shu, who comes from a middle-class background, but rejects her and condemns love as a sham: "Love, Miss, who has seen it? ... We have been deceived too long by this word.... People talk about love.... But who has seen it really work?... For me, I cannot stand it any longer; I don't want to hear the word 'love' anymore."[14] But in spite of himself, his affection for Miss Li continues to grow. Torn between his dedication to his work and his love for Miss Li, and aware that his tuberculosis is flaring up, he writes in his diary: "I cannot love, I have only hate. I hate all mankind. I hate myself.... If I cannot live for love, then I am willing to die for death. Only then can my hate disappear.''[15] He seeks to use ''the hatred that has been accumulated in the world'' and within himself to destroy the world, so that a new society can arise, and he is determined to use his life so as to arouse men's hatred for one another.[16]

His opportunity comes when an active union member, Chang Wei-ch'üan, is arrested and later decapitated by the authorities. To avenge Chang's death, Tu attempts to assassinate the garrison commander. But he only manages to wound his target slightly and commits suicide with his one remaining bullet. To Pa Chin, Tu's death represents a way to affirm life over death. What is more important to Pa Chin is that man need not be defeated — even though the choices may be extreme, man can find some way to assert his human spirit. Tu's death leads to the spiritual rebirth of his girl friend, Li Ching-shu, and of others. A month later Miss Li's house on Hai-ke Road is empty and the gate padlocked; several years later, there is a successful citywide strike of weavers in Shanghai, and its leader is none other than Miss Li.

The novel has many flaws. Pa Chin did not plan it as a coherent whole; instead he worked piecemeal, stringing together memories of his past and ideas obtained from what he had heard from friends. The effect, not surprisingly, is that in almost every chapter the tension falls as the author switches from one episode to the next, making no effort to consolidate the episodes into units as large as possible. The first main group of episodes, in the first two chapters, are meant to show examples of social injustice, but they include such unrelated elements as the automobile accident, Tu Ta-hsin's sophomoric poem, and scenes of street quarrels. The effectiveness of each scene is thus largely dissipated as the narrative fades back into Tu's recollection of events that took place four years ago. Similarly, Tu's growing love for Miss Li and his developing consciousness of his daemonic mission in life are split up into so many separate scenes and so often interrupted by much that is unnecessary (such as Yüan Jun-shen's recounting of his love affair in France) that the emotional force of Tu's romance and of his own self-hatred is weakened.

The primitiveness of Pa Chin's narrative technique is also reflected in his characterization and in the development of his thesis. What he has presented is a romantic who wants to become a martyr. By describing Tu as a man with an advanced case of tuberculosis, he lessens the significance of Tu's self-sacrifice in attempting to assassinate the garrison commander. And by elaborating on Tu's "mouthing" of ideas of love and hatred, he has portrayed Tu as an obsessed orator rather than as a man with burning inner discord. His other characters are equally disappointing. Li Ching-shu speaks of love in the abstract but seems devoid of any physical ardor; and her brother, Li Leng, remains too much a shadow in the background. Moreover, Pa Chin's thesis that society is unjust and hence deserves to be destroyed is not supported by factual details. He has simply failed to present convincingly the evils of the ruling class and the sufferings of the poor, or to explore the roots of social evil and the importance of collective action.

His prose is readable; its sentences follow a subject-and-predicate construction. Generally eschewing flourishes, he relies on a simple vocabulary and on downright plainness. Typical of his prose style is the following:

The street was usually quiet, but now suddenly it became busy. A crowd had gathered on the street. The people — of different sizes, wearing different styles of clothing, and having different faces — formed a large and compact circle. Those in the back craned their necks forward, as if straining to make their bodies several feet taller so that they could see what was happening in front of them. And those who were lucky enough to be standing in the front, seemed to be trying to expand their bodies, as if afraid that those standing behind them might steal a look at the scene before them. With the development of a "you-shove-me-and-I-shove-you" match, mixed with the noise made by the bystanders, the street had indeed become quite noisy and busy.[17]

Despite its obvious flaws, *Destruction* is made up of the usual themes, attitudes, and preoccupations of the Chinese novel of the 1920s. It expresses the hope that the time will come when "no one will ever cry, no one will ever suffer, every family will have its own house, every mouth will be fed, every person clothed and people will live in peace."[18] And it provides an initial probing of the Chinese intellectual's psyche in his quest to affirm life against the forces of negation.

Such a quest is elaborated with unexpected skill in *New Life,* which was meant to be another political novel about revolution. Even though the political theme differs little from that in *Destruction,* Pa Chin, almost against his own intention, succeeds in presenting a detailed study of a dangling revolutionary. Li Leng, the brother of Li Ching-shu in *Destruction,* is now the protagonist. A young man morbidly interested in himself, he is sanguinely detached from society and from the members of his own family, and even from those whom he loves deeply. His detachment becomes alienation, isolation from others and from his own self, until he finds himself again in the anarchist cause and heroically sacrifices himself.

As is Dostoevsky's *Notes from the Underground* (1864), *New Life* is written as a diary. It begins on a pessimistic and despairing note. Li Leng writes:

March 14

Still darkness and terror. My sister Ching and I returned to Shanghai not quite two months ago. Tu Ta-hsin has been dead for a year and a half. But he still lives in my heart; he continues to live there actively. Not only does he live in my heart, he also lives in my sister's heart.

Sister Ching, of course, still loves me; I also love her. I know that she loves no other man but me, but she has changed. She is remarkably different from what she was before. I am becoming a stranger to her. I know that what separates us is her belief in the [anarchist] cause, and that she gives a low priority to other things.

As for me, I have also changed. In the last year and a half, I haven't written a single poem or spoken one word in praise of beauty or nature. When I go over my old poems, they hardly seem to have been written by me. . . . Now when I pick up my pen to write poetry from time to time, the poems always revolve around the words "heh-an yü k'ung-pu" [darkness and terror]. . . .

I hate Tu Ta-hsin. My life used to be peaceful and happy. Ever since he entered it, ever since he opened a "new door to me," all has been misery and darkness. . . . Poverty and loneliness surround me. Sister Ching will soon leave me to work in a factory. She seems to be happy, because she has a cause to work for. But as for me, I have nothing.

My name is Li Leng, and my heart is cold. Darkness and terror surround me.[19]

Like Camus' Meursault in *The Stranger* (1942) or Saul Bellow's Joseph in *The Dangling Man* (1944), Li Leng is an alienated individual who encounters nothingness and sees life as absurd and meaningless: "For me, life is a great tragedy. No matter how we struggle and endure, the end result is destruction. And we must live before destruction arrives."[20] Moreover, he is caught up in a stifling ritual of daily activity and is highly susceptible to external stimuli. In a state of heightened consciousness he questions the very nature of human existence. He rebuts his sister's claim that "no one can live without living for a cause"[21] by answering that he has indeed so lived. He wonders why his mother continues to live under the tyrannical rule of his father; he doubts the usefulness of writing propaganda articles for a radical magazine or even of establishing such a magazine; and he questions the validity of the premise that any individual should sacrifice himself to save the world from destruction. Alienated from the world and from his own friends, he is accused of being an individualist. As the novel progresses he becomes increasingly aware that his struggle is to remain true to himself alone.

Filled with self-induced guilt, he loathes himself and heaps suffering and indignity on his head. Like Dostoevsky's Underground Man, Li is a self-alienated moral masochist. His disillusionment with people leads him to declare: "Except for myself, I am responsible for no one," and he asks: "Where has my life gone? How can I recover the life I once had? Why should I have a memory? It brings me pain."[22]

Like the Underground Man, he talks about himself. Living in a tiny room in Shanghai, he seems pleased with his wretchedness — he recites in detail all his disgusting traits, all his frustrations. In his April 11 entry he writes:

> Loneliness and depression. Darkness and death...
> No friend came to visit me.
> Sister Ching did not respond to my letter.
> Is it because she didn't have time or is it because
>   she has forgotten my existence?
> I cannot forget either her or Wen-ju.
> Anxiety, worry. Is it true that there is no end to
>   suffering?[23]

His imagined isolation is the other side of his gigantic idealism. He thinks that his parents, his sister, his lover Wen-ju, and his friends are all morally and mentally inferior to him. It is largely because they cannot see the world from his point of view that he hates them and himself as well.

He seeks to suffer. First, just by writing the diary he chooses to lacerate himself, though at the same time to comfort himself by admitting the nature of the wound. Second, he desires not to achieve. He prefers sitting in his room doing nothing to either joining his friends in working for a magazine or his sister and his girl friend, Wen-ju, in organizing a labor union. Third, like Bellow's Joseph, he is filled with guilt feelings. He revels in and derives pleasure from hearing his sister's denunciation of him: "Leng, why don't you follow me? Isn't my love sufficient to save you from your hollow individualism? I can never understand why you must continue to tread the path of destruction. We can't leave you in darkness, to let you be destroyed." After this tongue-lashing, he muses: "Hollow individualism. The path to destruction. Why did she use these expressions to criticize me? Why couldn't she spare me, allow me to tread my own path?"[24]

Again like Bellow's Joseph, he longs for the innocent world of his childhood, one untainted by the death of Tu Ta-hsin. As his girl friend, Wen-ju, fondles his hair, he reminisces: "I feel I have returned to my childhood. After I had been mistreated by other children, I often wept on Mother's bosom. She would comfort me; she would fondle my hair. Her hand was so gentle, very much like Wen-ju's is now. That hand and that soft bosom were a safe harbor during my childhood, one like Wen-ju provides now."[25] But the truth is different. Wen-ju cannot replace his mother's love or lift him out of despair, even though he tries to love her and to develop faith in mankind through her.

Unlike Dostoevsky's Underground Man, who has no way to escape from himself, either when he is alone or when he is with others, either through thought or through action, Li lifts himself from the abyss of despair by voluntarily joining and working for a labor union in Amoy. Here in a way similar to Bellow's Joseph, who joins the army, Li gives up his old self — death of the self; like Tu Ta-hsin before him, he attempts to assassinate the chief of police and is arrested and sentenced to death. While in prison he dreams of his mother, who endorses his action fully: "My son, don't forget that we were not brought into this world as ornaments to peace. We are not in this world to receive but to give. We ourselves may never have received any love, but we must share our love with others...."[26] Having established his "peace" with and received blessings from his mother, he faces and welcomes death with resignation and without fear: "My death will bring me a new life. I shall find my new life in mankind's self-improvement."[27]

Olga Lang considers the description of Li Leng's despair intolerably long;[28] however, that is exactly where the strength of the novel lies — in its successful presentation of a Chinese "dangling man": the masochistic sufferer, despairing and alienated. As was pointed out above, it invites comparison with Dostoevsky's *Notes from the Underground* and, of course, with Bellow's *Dangling Man.*

The artistic achievement of *New Life* was not to be repeated in *Li-na,* the story of a Russian revolutionary's birth, life, and exile to Siberia during the 1870s. Written in the epistolary form, the novelette contains nineteen letters, addressed to one Yuliana. In the letters Li-na's conversion from an upper-class lady to a revolutionary is slowly unfolded; in them she attacks the Tsar and his policies, the starvation of the newly freed serfs, and the corruption existing in the church, the military, and in other branches of government. But most important, the letters reveal her love for a nihilist activist who is exiled to Siberia. The novelette's format required that Pa Chin be faithful to the style in which he thought a Russian would write letters to her girl friend. Consequently, the prose is awkward and often reads like a stiff and literal translation.

IV   The Love Trilogy: *A Modern Handbook of Personal Conduct*

Pa Chin said he was fond of *The Love Trilogy* because many of its characters were based on the lives of his friends. Many of his friends were caught between parental demands and personal preferences in marital affairs and in conflicts between work and love. To answer their questions, Pa Chin wrote the trilogy not only for his friends but also for anyone who might have similar problems. Hence, he uses his characters to voice his points of view. For example, in *Fog,* his moral is that the young must choose their own mate and he illustrates this thesis by telling the story of Chou Ju-shui.

Writer Chou Ju-shui meets the beautiful Miss Chang Jo-lan at a seashore hotel. Attracted to each other, they discuss their goals in life, their love of nature, and even their attachment to their mothers. However, Chou is afraid to express his love to Chang because he is married. At seventeen, his parents had arranged for him to marry an illiterate woman who gave him a son a year later. Shortly after his marriage, he left home to study in Peking and Japan for nine years and has not been home since. Though in love with Miss Chang, he is tormented by his conflicting obligations to the wife he does not love, the son he does not know, the parents he does not wish to offend, and the beautiful girl friend he does not wish to lose.

To help solve Chou's problems, Pa Chin introduces Ch'en Chen and Wu Jen-min. Both liberals, they urge Chou either to live with

Chang or to marry her. But Chou gives a typical Chinese son's answer: "Wouldn't this embarass my parents? Wouldn't this mean a complete break with my family? Never to see them again? This would be too cruel."[29] His answer provokes Ch'en Chen's emotional outburst against parents and conscience:

Conscience, do away with it. I don't want it. I want everyone to be punished for his errors, regardless of who commits them.... To bring a baby into the world, to place hope before him, to tempt him with that hope, and then to take that hope away from him at the last minute and replace it with hell.... Parents who would do this must be punished.... And yet you feel you should sacrifice yourself for them, you want to hide behind the shield of conscience and evade your responsibilities toward society and mankind. Truly, you are a coward.[30]

Of course, to Pa Chin the correct option for Chou would be to follow Ch'en's advice. But Chou lacks the courage to accept Miss Chang's love; if to do so he has to reject his parents. A year later, at the same seashore hotel, a much sadder Chou reads a letter from his father. It says: "Your wife died of illness more than two years ago. Worried that you might be upset, I didn't tell you. After the news of your return came out this year, many families with eligible daughters became interested in you. Since I'm getting old and have been accused of being too old-fashioned, I will not meddle in your marriage this time. You can decide the matter after you return home...."[31] It seems that Chou has never returned home as he originally intended to do; as a result, his conscience and cowardice cost him the woman he wanted.

In *Rain,* Pa Chin shifts his attention to the problem of love versus duty, one which had plagued his earlier revolutionaries and possibly many of his friends. Consider, for instance, Tu Ta-hsin in *Destruction.* To Tu, love and revolutionary work are incompatible. Regarding his relationship with Miss Li Ching-shu, he asks himself again and again: "Why must I love her? Why am I still in love with her? Haven't I sworn not to love any woman? My responsibility ... is to destroy that world."[32] A similar conflict torments Wu Jen-min in *Rain.* Having recently lost his wife, he is despondent. Torn by internal conflicts, he has doubts about his own revolutionary work and that of his comrades. Unwilling to accept Miss Cheng Yü-wen's love for him and unable to keep Chih-chun, a former student and admirer of his, he wallows in self-pity. As the novel drags to an end, Wu concludes: "Love is a game for the leisurely class. I have no right to it. I am only sorry that love has blinded me and given me so much trouble."[33]

In *Lightning,* Pa Chin presents a solution to the problem of love versus duty. In Li P'ei-chu, he has created a Chinese woman revolutionary who is similar to the Russian Vera Figner.[34] Miss Li is a counselor, mother, and companion to her comrades and a lover to Wu Jen-min. It is she who articulates Pa Chin's thoughts on the subject: "Love is not a sin, not something to be ashamed of. I love him [Wu] and he loves me. So both he and I are happy. Tomorrow maybe we will both die; why can't you allow us to have a little happiness today? Love can only give us courage...."[35] It is also through Miss Li's love for Wu that Wu becomes a responsible and effective leader in *Lightning.* He represents Pa Chin's ideal man who has found the happy combination of commitment to revolution and satisfaction of his personal needs. Thus, in the trilogy Pa Chin provides the young and the revolutionaries with his guidelines for personal conduct.

Also in the trilogy, Pa Chin presents a new generation of Chinese women. Miss Ch'in Yün-yü in *Fog* is fashionably dressed and educated. She can talk fluently about literature and about her personal philosophy of life, and she speaks of love as the cure for all social evils.[36] Miss Chang Jo-lan is another recently liberated woman. When Chou Ju-shui tells her that he has a wife and child at home, she replies without hesitation: "Whether you have a wife or not makes no difference to me. True love transcends all these obstacles. I love you and know you also love me. Consequently all problems will disappear."[37] Her view is a radical departure from the traditional one which frowned upon liaisons with married men. In *Rain* there are two women ready to sacrifice themselves for love. After discovering that she could not have Wu Jen-min for herself, Miss Chen Yü-wen commits suicide. And Chih Chun decides to sacrifice her happiness and marry a government official to save Wu from arrest by the government authorities. These women see love as a new ingredient in life, one which they would defend and further at all costs.

Moving away from the sanctity of love, Pa Chin touches briefly on sexual needs. In traditional Chinese fiction, women were expected to be virtuous and were taught to stifle their sexual feelings and to accept the fallacy that they were created with a "normal" attitude of sexual indifference; the *Biographies of Illustrious Women* projects as positive female images wise mothers, virtuous wives, and chaste widows. Women were seldom seen as having sexual desires of their own. Those who did were considered to be threats to male well-being and a direct cause of male destruction. An example of this is expressed in the celebrated *Chin P'ing Mei* (*The Golden Lotus*), in which the heroine's insatiable desire for sex brings not only destruction to her men but, in the end, her own grisly death. But with the increasing awareness of women as human beings that followed the May Fourth Movement, writers wrote about true love, marriage, and sexual relationships. For example, Ting Ling flaunted sexual restiveness in "Meng k'o" and in "The Diary of Miss Sophia" (collected in her first volume of short stories entitled *In the Darkness* and published in 1928) and in her novella called "Wei Hu" (1930).[38]

A modest man, other than in describing a character's attitude toward free love, Pa Chin seldom makes direct reference to sexual relationships, and his descriptions of love-making rarely go beyond kissing and light petting.[39] However, an exception can be found in *Thunder,* in which he seems to acknowledge the reality of physical passion. *Thunder* is a novelette about a group of young revolutionaries who live together and share much of what they possess. Among the women is Hui, who believes in free love and, in the following dialogue, affirms the importance and the reality of physical passion; whereas Te, the young man with whom she is speaking, holds traditional moral views and argues that sex is bad for him and for everyone else:

"You have done Min in, now you want to do me in. I'm not afraid. Just remember I'm thunder, thunder."

"Min? How did I do him in? What we did was by mutual consent. Now, that's ended."

The two pairs of eyes stared at each other. They were like two beasts, awaiting a chance to devour each other.

Time passed in silence, then Hui spoke: "Te, let's make peace with each other. Why must we act as though we hated each other? What good does it do?"

"But, ..." Te said, torn by internal conflicts and looking away from her, "our work has been ruined many times by women. Now ... you frolicked with Min and others, but I'm not like Min."...

"But that's not woman's fault. Both sexes are responsible," Hui explained gently. "Sex is a natural instinct, a human desire. We have a duty to satisfy that desire...."[40]

What Hui affirms is women's right to sex, and that sex is not bad.

What she has expressed is not new to a Western reader but it must have been shocking for her Chinese readers in the 1930s.

If the trilogy is considered primarily as a guidebook for personal conduct, its success in presenting clear-cut answers to the questions troubling the young is decidedly limited. And as literature, it must be considered a failure. Interested only in providing answers to questions, Pa Chin pays little attention to literary requirements. He passes up opportunities to describe settings and gives no evocation of place. Manipulating a set of predictable circumstances such as Ch'en Chen's death in an automobile accident in *Rain* and the unsuccessful assassination attempt on the life of the garrison commander in *Lightning,* he simply rehashes incidents he has already used in *Destruction.* The plot in *Fog* never lifts itself off the ground; those in *Rain* and *Thunder* are overly melodramatic; and the one in *Lightning* offers little excitement. His revolutionaries, as always, are too emotional and his description of social evils nonexistent. His lovers, as typified by Wu Jen-min, Li P'ei-chu, and others, are wooden puppets used merely to illustrate different points of view. These novels contain neither the suffering nor the ecstasy one usually associates with love stories. And, regrettably, the daemonic force of sex is left largely unexplored.

V *Portrait of a Lady*

Inspired by his eldest brother's unhappy marriage and suicide, Pa Chin wrote *Family* and *Autumn in Spring. Family,* together with *Spring* and *Autumn,* is an indictment of the archaic Chinese family system and will be discussed in a separate chapter; *Autumn in Spring* is also an indictment of the system. The theme is established early in the book. Teacher Lin has just received a telegram informing him that his elder brother has committed suicide, and that he left a note before taking his life. The note reads: "Marriage without choice, conjugal union without love, old traditional concepts.... My happiness has been destroyed by them all. Why should I continue to live for them?"[41] Teacher Lin fares little better than his brother and will also suffer the pangs of unrequited love.

The theme of unrequited love caused by parental interference is commonplace, but *Autumn in Spring* was written with artistry. The scenes, alternating between the intoxicating bliss of courtship and feelings of doom, are often nearly perfect. In a clear and straightforward manner, Teacher Lin describes a typical scene between himself and his student-lover, Yün:

Yes, she was by my side. Yet her heart and mine were quite far apart. But how far apart our hearts really were, I did not know.

"Love is a beautiful thing. It is so beautiful, but it's not for me," she whispered, as if talking to herself. Her voice was soft and melancholy, like that of a violin.

I looked at her face, which seemed to be shrouded in fog. The fog made her look even more attractive; it was like a bride's veil. But this bride would not belong to me.

I embraced her carefully and tenderly, as if holding something very precious. I was crying; drop by drop, the tears fell on her hair and glistened like pearls.

"You're crying," she said, raising her head. She smiled. That smile, I thought, was so much prettier than tears. She pressed her finger against my lips, and then quickly kissed me on the mouth. The kiss came suddenly, like a flash of lightning.

I wanted to return her kiss, but she turned her head away.

"Yün, you behave so strangely today, you have changed," I said, in pain. "Tell me what's wrong."[42]

Yün never tells Lin what is wrong but encourages him to think only of the pleasures of the moment. Among Pa Chin's female characters, Yün is more complex than most and, in a certain way, romantically quixotic and duty-conscious, torn between free love and duty. A liberated woman, she delights in physical manifestations of her love for Lin, and yet, upon learning that her mother is ailing, she is overcome by her sense of duty and returns home to take care of her; and when her father insists that she not see Lin anymore, she romantically exaggerates duty so that it means obeying her father's wishes, right or wrong, and writes to Lin to terminate their relationship. But when she becomes ill, she purposely fails to take the proper medicine and dies shortly afterwards. In contrast to the diffident Lin, she seems to be self-assured and forever courting catastrophe. Where Lin will offer anything for the sake of peace and marriage, she must torment him and herself to indulge her childish love of melodrama. Alternately cold and wild, passionate and detached, but always self-absorbed, she cares little about what her love means to Lin and never tries to salvage anything of their relationship.

However much Pa Chin may have wanted to demonstrate the evils of the family system, this novelette defies his wish. Yün's family is no more responsible for the unhappy ending than is Lin's family. Contrary to Pa Chin's wishes, the novelette stands out as a character study of Yün, a young Chinese girl who has found romantic love fascinating, parental obedience obligatory, and self-sacrifice necessary.

VI   *"Foreigners, Go Home!"*

Hostility toward foreigners started to grow after the Opium War and came to a climax in the Boxer Rebellion of 1900. One of the charges against the Manchus was that they had failed to protect China against foreign imperialism and had given away too much territory, money, and sovereignty. But immediately before and during the revolution of 1911, both the revolutionaries and the Manchus took pains not to antagonize the foreign powers inasmuch as each group feared the foreigners might support the opposite side. Consequently, after the revolution the foreigners and their interests in China were well protected. Their factories, producing cheap manufactured goods for sale in China and elsewhere, were visible in major cities. Having access to cheap labor and low-priced raw materials, they made huge profits, often at the expense of the backward Chinese.[43] Hence, antiforeignism was popular during the early years of the twentieth century. For example, a revolutionary from Hunan, Ch'en T'ien-hua (1875–1905), wrote of threats of foreign powers in his *Chin-shih chung* (*A Bell to Warn the World*) and *Meng hui-t'ou* (*About Face*).[44]

Pa Chin wrote *The Setting Sun* to express a similar theme. Using a realistic-symbolic approach, his tale of the evil doings of foreigners in China has a great emotional impact on the reader. The novel begins with a realistic description of the wanton and bloody shooting of defenseless Chinese demonstrators protesting against foreign-controlled factories in Shanghai on May 30, 1925. To explore further the problem of economic exploitation of the workers, the scene shifts from Shanghai to Nanking. Wu Yang-ch'ing, a college student who witnessed the massacre on Nanking Road, goes to Nanking to help organize protest meetings. Subsequently students and workers stage a strike against the Yi-chi factory, a foreign-owned enterprise. At a meeting between labor and management, the former receives no concessions but only insults from the latter, culminating in an ugly incident in which an Englishman slaps the face of a Chinese labor representative. This touches off another round of protests.

Shifting from the realistic level to the symbolic, Pa Chin describes a dream which Wu has. In the dream, a tall Caucasian bluntly and arrogantly tells Wu: "...to handle all you dirty monsters, I feel we should not use diplomats but allied troops who would pillage you, abuse you, rape you, and slaughter you, so that you would fear foreigners for generations to come. With our latest handling of you, maybe we have achieved a ten-year truce period."[45]

The novel expresses the accumulated anger of a frustrated people living under foreign domination. One little boy vows that he will fight the foreign devils when he grows up; an adult wonders why the Chinese soldiers are no match for foreign troops and why the foreigners kill Chinese with such complete abandonment.[46] Shying away from offering realistic solutions to China's problems with the foreigners, Pa Chin merely suggests the need for active resistance by the Chinese.

The same theme appears in *Dream on the Sea*. Pa Chin calls it a child's tale, and the action takes place on the deck of a ship crossing the Mediterranean. To an attentive listener, a mysterious woman tells her life story. Her country was dominated by a foreign enemy who had the support of the native upper classes. Even though she was from the upper class, she and her husband joined the lower classes, who were really slaves, in waging endless warfare against the enemy. Her husband was arrested and killed, but she continued to be active in the underground movement. Very much fascinated by the woman's story, the listener looks but can find no trace of her the next day.

The novel allegorizes Japan's political and military encroachment on China. The foreign enemy here is Japan, which presumably acts with the support of the Chinese business class and the tacit approval of the Chinese government; the lower classes are the millions of Chinese enslaved by the Japanese; and the woman's efforts to overthrow the enemy represent the Chinese people's heroic efforts in resisting the Japanese. Artistically weak, *Dream on the Sea* is a piece of propaganda literature.

VII *Death City*

The Setting Sun ends on an upbeat note, as Wu Yang-ch'ing mulls over the death of Wang Hsüeh-li, a worker who has sacrificed his life. Wu believes that Wang "has not died. Wang is a setting sun. IIis death is temporary, ... he will once again rise like the dawning sun of the next day, and will shine on mankind with the rays of a new life."[47] But in *The Antimony Miners* the sun seems forever submerged in darkness. The novel takes place in "Death City," which is described as follows:

Located in a valley, Death City lies quietly between two mountains. Of course, Death City is not its original name, but the miners have called it that for so long that they have forgotten its real name.

In the morning, Death City is quiet. There are only a few pedestrians, each dressed in blue, on the gravel road.... Weary, they have nothing much to say, and make no loud noises.

Here it is difficult to see sunshine. It is always cloudy, the sky grayish. People are used to the weather and don't particularly dislike it. Of course, when the sun is out, there seems to be more going on, and the people seem happier. But these occasions are rare. Hence people often sigh and say: "Death City!"[48]

The novel is intended to be an exposé of the evils of the capitalist system, echoing Proudhon's aphorism: "property is theft" and collectivist Alexander Berkman's idea that "The wealth the workers have created ... has indeed been stolen from them. And they are being robbed in the same way every day of their lives, even at this very moment."[49] The novel describes Death City and the dreary existence of the miners, and draws a sharp distinction between the miners (all good) and mine owners (all evil).

Lured to the mines by promises of high wages, the ignorant miners are soon told that they have been paid the fabulous sum of five hundred silver dollars and are therefore contracted to work for the company for five years. In fact, they have only received five dollars each. To prevent them from escaping, the management chains them with foot shackles at night, feeds them a subsistence diet, has them watched by armed guards, and subjects them to torture and shooting. The novel ends with a cave-in which kills many miners, but the company suffers no loss. It hires more miners and continues to make tens of thousands of dollars which are deposited in the owners' bank accounts.

To add human interest to the novel, Pa Chin includes the story of one worker, Shen-yi. He went to work in the mine thinking that he could make enough money there to redeem his girl friend from bondage as a maidservant in a rich man's family. But he dies in the cave-in. Meanwhile, she "continued to labor for her owners, tor-

tured by her heavy workload every day. But she never neglected to
pray to the gods to protect her Shen-yi so that he could come home
soon with the money to redeem her. Of course, her prayers
wouldn't go on forever. Within a year she died of exhaustion, and
on her dying lips she softly whispered a man's name. Her soft cries
were not heard by others. Even if they had been, no one would have
shed a tear for her . . . ''[50]

While *The Antimony Miners* may be oversimplified in its handling of economic issues, melodramatic in plot, and weak in
characterization, Pa Chin's intention is to show that the miner is
crushed, starved, ignorant, and suffering, and, more funda-
mentally, to present the socialist and anarchist view of the classic
struggle between labor and capital. In *Snow,* however, he
attempted to present a more sophisticated version of the pit "where
there is no light, no change of seasons, no flowers, no wind but
eternal darkness. . . . ''[51]

In writing *Snow,* Pa Chin was aware of Zola's *Germinal* (1855).
While Zola placed much emphasis on the effects of both heredity
and environment on his characters, Pa Chin ignored the first and
concentrated on the second. Like Zola, he was interested in telling
his reader about working conditions in the mines and how the
miners and their families lived, while keeping the action constantly
moving and introducing a number of people, each of whom represents a different aspect of a miner's life.

It is not a pleasant picture. The married miners have a hard time
making ends meet and the single ones squander their hard-earned
dollars in gambling dens and brothels. Even though there are more
than three thousand workers, they have no effective leadership and
are under constant and relentless pressure to increase their produc-
tion. There is no escape from life in the mine. An elderly worker
comments that once a person goes to work in a mine, it is like
having sold his life to it. Another worker, with more than ten years
service, is summarily dismissed when his health becomes a problem. Shortly afterwards he commits suicide. And when the workers
begin to organize to stage a strike, they are shot by the guards and
suppressed by government troops. The fifteenth anniversary of the
mine's founding degenerates into a massacre.

While Zola did not allow his political enthusiasms to blind him to
psychological realities and a sense of fairness, unfortunately Pa
Chin's deep emotional involvement with ideological causes costs
him his objectivity and the ability to develop psychologically con-

vincing characters. For example, to Zola, the struggle at Matsou is not simply a revolt of oppressed and innocent workers against wicked and tyrannous employers; it is more accurately a clash of financial interests. Zola's employers are not devils, nor are his employees angels. In fact, one of the managers, Hennebeau, has terrible personal worries, and his livelihood depends upon his carrying out the policy of the board of directors. Another man, Deneulin, faces ruin and humiliation after having sunk all his money into modern improvements in his mine, and he is even respected by his workers. All are victims of the distant, anonymous power crouching, as Zola says, like some malignant god in his impenetrable shrine. In Pa Chin's *Snow,* the reader does not find such an exposition of both sides; he sees good associated only with the underdog and evil only with the mine managers. By failing to develop his characters convincingly, Pa Chin makes *Snow* into just another political pamphlet containing all the half-truths, exaggerations, and oversimplifications familiar to works of propaganda.

VIII *Anarchist Ideas*

Pa Chin knew anarchism well. During his childhood in Chengtu, he wrote for anarchist magazines, and by the time he wrote *Destruction* in 1927, he had already been exposed to different anarchist writings, including those of Alexander Berkman, Bakunin, Kropotkin, Enrico Malatesta, Emma Goldman, Pierre Joseph Proudhon, Vanzetti, and the Chicago anarchists.[52] He gave himself the pen name "Pa Chin," openly professed his admiration for Emma Goldman, often identified himself as an anarchist, and used several anarchistic ideas in his early novels.

First, he sought to portray his society as unjust. In *Destruction,* he attempted unsuccessfully to reveal economic and social injustices and, through one of Tu Ta-hsin's poems, the sufferings of the rural poor.[53] In *The Antimony Miners* and *Snow* he concentrates on the plight of miners, and in *The Setting Sun,* on the problems of factory workers in foreign-owned industries. All these novels show how important and urgent a radical examination of the existing social structure was, in his view.

Second, he stresses the need for action by emphasizing the gulf that exists between rich and poor, the former being heartless and the latter inert. For instance, he uses as an example Hsü Ch'iu-shan, the wife of a young engineer in *Snow.* She advises her husband to recommend that the management establish a school for workers' children and take other steps to improve the miners' conditions; when her husband suggests such programs to the management, he is ridiculed. The only alternative, it seems to Pa Chin, is the strike and other forms of militancy. In *Snow,* the clerk Chao instigates the workers to rebel openly against management's oppressive rule, and so do Tu Ta-hsin in *Destruction,* Li Leng in *New Life,* and Wang Hsüeh-li in *The Setting Sun.*

Third, he approves of violence, including assassination. Like Kropotkin, who refused to condemn vengeance as a motive for political violence,[54] Pa Chin's martyrs (such as Tu Ta-shin, Li Leng, and Te) are motivated by personal grudge as well as by a desire to defy society. They show the people what they believe to be the only way to a better future and to the abolition of economic and political slavery. They typify, to Pa Chin, those who carry on "propaganda of the deed."

Fourth, unlike the Proudhonists, who "opposed the entry of nonworkers into the General Council of the First International and generally objected to the presence of educated bourgeois in the labor movement,"[55] Pa Chin sees a role for the educated. In *Rain,* young intellectuals cooperate with workers in bringing about a revolution. They submerge themselves in the workers' organizations, publish articles and newspapers, and arouse the revolutionary aspirations of the workers. Their formula is reminiscent of the Russian populist concept of "fusing with the people," which the Bakunists of the Russian movement favored in the mid-1870s.[56]

Fifth, although Pa Chin grants intellectuals a role in revolutionary activities, he stresses the masses as the primary factor in a revolt. To him, the people already possess an instinct for revolution; intellectuals have to understand how the revolutionary potential of the masses actually functions and how to encourage its expression. They ought not attempt to direct or control the people's drive to rebellion. He maintains unquestioned faith in the revolutionary instinct of the masses and assumes that they will know what tactics to employ during an actual revolution. Further, he assumes that, with only occasional errors, they will be able to run a new and just society.

In short, Pa Chin's early political novels describe a society sharply divided between rich and poor, in which only political revolution can bring about the abolition of social injustice. His major objective is to evoke, through his works, sympathy for the suffering masses. He attacks those in power as greedy, immoral, and oppressive in contrast to the invariably virtuous poor. With ideology dominating his works, he manipulates his characters with a ruthless insistence that they conform to his will and that they illuminate prefabricated themes rather than fulfill their inner possibilities. Consequently, many fade into abstractions. His methods are primitive, but the public he wrote for had not yet developed even the fundamentals of literary discrimination; they preferred clear-cut dividing lines between good and evil. And if nothing else, they found their feelings and aspirations articulated fully, if not always artistically, by Pa Chin.

CHAPTER 3

Early Short Stories

BETWEEN 1927 and 1936 Pa Chin completed the following volumes of short stories: *Fu-ch'ou* (*Revenge*), *Kuang-ming* (*Light*), *Tien-yi* (*The Electric Chair*), *Mo-pu* (*The Dustcloth*), *Chiang-chün* (*The General*), *Ch'en-mo* (*Deep Silence*), *Ch'en-lo* (*Sinking Down*), *Shen, kuei, jen* (*God, Ghost, Man*), *Ch'en-mo II* (*Deep Silence II*), *Fa ti ku-shih* (*Story of Hair*), and *Chang-sheng t'a* (*Pagoda of Long Life*).

Discussing the formative influences on his short stories, Pa Chin cited his exposure to the works of Maupassant, Pushkin, Chekhov, Gorki, George Sand, and Lu Hsün, as well as to Chinese opera; he insisted that what he had learned from these writers and the opera was the expression of genuine sentiments.[1] Since he classified China as a country whose people were oppressed, he chose to write about revolutionaries, exiles, the dispossessed, and the intellectuals in his short stories as he did in his novels; even in the fables he wrote in *Pagoda of Long Life* he always tried to convey a clear political message to his readers. But in addition to politics, he also wrote about the lives of ordinary people.

In discussing the writing of short stories, he maintained that he did not learn literary techniques from other writers and that he was, in fact, a writer without any technique to speak of. A casual reader of Pa Chin's early short stories may well agree with his assessment and dismiss his short stories as lacking in artistry. But more patient readers will probably discover that Pa Chin is a fine short-story-teller, capable of using many techniques to illuminate the human condition, that he offers variety in structure, in points of view, in plot development, in characterization, in setting, and in his use of language.

This does not mean that all his short stories are good, for in fact he is an uneven writer. At his worst, his flaws are glaring: political propaganda, puppet-characters, and predictable plot development dominate; at his best, however, his strengths are also apparent: he involves the reader emotionally with his characters by showing why they behave as they do, by displaying traits that resemble the reader's own, and by stirring the reader's sense of what it means to be human.

An examination of some of his short stories, arranged by subject matter, is the focus of this chapter.

I *Revolutionaries*

In general, Pa Chin's revolutionaries belong to two types. The first are idealistic and heroic, and the second less of both but more human. For example, in "Tsai men-chien shang" ("On the Threshold"), the narrator is ostensibly concerned with telling the reader about the activities of an elderly Frenchman and his young daughter in the French revolutionary underground movement, their participation in the Spanish civil war, and their execution; in *Deep Silence II* Pa Chin glamorizes Jean Paul Marat, Georges Jacques Danton, and Maximilien de Robespierre, three figures of the French Revolution; in "Story of Hair" and in "Yü" ("Rain") he romanticizes the struggle of several Koreans against the Japanese and the disappearance and execution of a woman revolutionary. As an outsider who had never participated in a revolution but who admired those who did, his attitude toward revolutionaries was worshipful. Consequently, his revolutionaries are always larger than life, and therefore unconvincing; some of his stories about them succeed as well-written fictional biographies, but others are merely propaganda pieces.

However, in "Yi-ko nü-jen" ("A Woman"), Pa Chin shifts his emphasis from abstract revolutionary fervor to the problems faced by a former revolutionary. Using a third-person omniscient point of view, he describes the woman, as the story unfolds, by imagining in detail her every move:

Next-door's wall clock struck nine times. She, somewhat startled, raised her head, stopped her sewing, shifted her gaze from her work to the door. The door was partially opened — no one was pushing it. She listened and heard no footsteps on the staircase. Listening some more, she did not hear anyone knocking on the downstairs door either.

She heaved a sigh, wrinkled her eyebrows somewhat, then turned her head to look at the bed. Her child, now nearly three, was sleeping soundly with his head on the pillow, a smile on his tiny face. She looked at his face for a while and then smiled. She lowered her head and resumed her sewing.[2]

Then Pa Chin tells his reader: "She was a woman who loved to think. Her thoughts oftentimes shifted from one subject to the next, to another and still to another. Yet, she very seldom reminisced about her past, especially not about one particular period of her life. She had almost buried the memories of that period...."[3]

Having delineated the woman through description and editorial comment, Pa Chin shifts his attention to the plot, which is slight. The woman's husband, a few minutes after the above scene, returns home with a former colleague of hers. After some polite chit-chat about their former work and their friends, she frankly tells the visitor: "My spirits have been low lately, and I literally do not want to leave the house. Your situation and mine are different, and there is nothing to say even when I see my former friends."[4]

To show the protagonist's complete transformation from a revolutionary to a housewife, Pa Chin uses a conversation between her and her husband after the friend has left. Gently she asks him if he has borrowed the money to pay the rent; and when he tells her that he has quit his job and has only five *yüan* left, she murmurs: "Rent, twelve *yüan,* milk bill, four *yüan* and thirty cents. How is this five *yüan* going to be enough.... Tomorrow...."[5]

What distinguishes this unidentified woman from Pa Chin's other revolutionaries is her ordinariness. No longer mouthing slogans, she soberly tries to face up to an unemployed husband, to economic hardship, and to her family's survival. Having only minimal plot development, the story is more like a sketch, and what success it has lies partly in Pa Chin's method of narration which, after presenting the protagonist to the reader, follows with authorial comments about her, her conversation with the guest, and lastly, her monologue. As a result, she comes through as a person, not a caricature.

While "A Woman" is but a sketch of a former revolutionary, "Hua-hsüeh ti jih-tzu" ("The Days When the Snow Melts") seeks to lay bare the psyche of a newly converted revolutionary. The story takes place in France. Describing himself as a person who loves the sun, the snow, the wind, the mountains, and everything else, the narrator tells what he knows about a certain Chinese couple. They are, to him, ideally suited for each other: young, handsome, and financially well-to-do; yet he finds them frequently quarreling over trivia and the husband unreasonably testy. One day in a private conversation with the husband, he learns that the latter is enamored of a new political belief, plans to return to China to participate in revolutionary work, and has been deliberately making himself disagreeable to his wife to minimize her sense of loss when she is eventually left behind. The narrator tries, unsuccessfully, to reason with the husband and, to his horror, the husband even suggests that the narrator take "an interest" in the wife, a proposal that is rejected out of hand. Not long afterwards, he learns that the couple has returned to China. Four years later, while sunbathing on a beach in the south of France, he accidentally meets the wife, who is now married to a young, handsome, and considerate man, and he learns from her that her former husband is still working in China.

The story is interesting in its portrayal of the husband's psyche. At the least, he is to be remembered for the methodical steps by which he tried to alienate himself from his wife; at best, he is to be admired as a purist who sees no compromise possible between family and revolutionary work. On the other hand, the narrator is also interesting. While ostensibly telling the reader about someone else, he reveals a great deal about himself. With his sunny disposition, he represents the average mind, and humanity as a whole. He cannot see under the surface and has no communication with the husband. Incapable of understanding the husband's motive, he naturally views him as a driven man and an escapist, running away from the challenges of normal human life.

II *Exiles*

Exile is one of Pa Chin's favorite themes. As a student in Paris he met many Russian Jews and refugees of other nationalities. Sympathetic to them, he tells their stories again and again. For instance, "Wang-ming" ("Exile") is about an antifascist Italian refugee called Fabiani, who declares that his heart belongs only to his native Italy and who finds life in Paris vexing; Pa Chin's two stories about Yuliana Volberg ("Yali-an-na" and "Yali-an-na Wu-po-erh-ko") give detailed accounts of Yuliana's childhood and youth in Poland, her participation in the anarchist movement, her deportation from France, and her death from tuberculosis in Poland.

But it is in "Chiang-chün" ("The General") that Pa Chin most effectively uses the exile theme. He makes the reader feel the anguish of exile through the experiences of a White Russian officer living in Shanghai, who tries not to lose his identity in a world that will always be alien to him. Pa Chin's technique is to make the reader see — partly through the Russian's illusions about himself and partly through the realities of the Russian's life — the true sadness of being an exile.

Unwanted in his native and now Communist Russia and unable to adjust to life in China, the "general" lives a lonely and frustrating life. To relieve the drabness of the present, he dreams about the bygone days in St. Petersburg, about how he courted his wife Anna, and about the parties in St. Petersburg at which generals, their wives, and daughters danced to soft music. Now spending most of his time in a Chinese café, he tells his story again and again to an unappreciative waiter, while simultaneously making strenuous efforts to preserve in an alien world an identity based on the tastes and feelings of far-off St. Petersburg. In his old-fashioned and humorless way, he never conceives of the possibility of changing his way of thinking. He sees his own attitudes as being completely natural — including his bad temper and his hatred of everything Chinese. To the fat Chinese waiter at the café he bellows: "Over here in your country nothing is right, even dogs don't bite, they have become so meek."[6] Resorting to national chauvinism to assert his superiority, he dismisses winter in China as not frigid enough, the wind not fierce enough, and the country a vast desert inhabited by lifeless people. In short, even though Russia's beauty may be matchless anywhere, it is pointless to argue with him. In reminiscing he is interested only in sentiment, not in facts. To enhance his illusions, he insists to the affable Chinese waiter that he be addressed as "General," even though he was never more than a first-lieutenant in the Russian army, and he pretends that his nightly walk home is that of a general returning to his mansion.

"Home" is a sparsely furnished room on the second floor of an apartment building; "home" is the sad reality of being an exile as he listens to his wife's nightly tales of horror at the hands of drunken customers and to her fervent wish to return to Mother Russia. Unable to face the fact that his wife is a whore who supports him with her earnings, he returns to the safe haven — the café — only to be told by the insensitive waiter that once upon a time another Russian exile had frequently come to the café and emptied a bag of Russian soil on his table while the waiter wondered at the Russian's weird behavior. Reminded of his own situation, the "general" staggers out of the café; his pathos is not complete until the last scene of the story, when he drunkenly insists to a Chinese constable that he is a Russian general. And as he lies on the ground, he seems to see an American sailor mounting his wife. His pretensions gone, he opens his eyes and murmurs: "Take me to her, take me to Anna! I must tell her I've decided to return to Russia."[7]

With a master stroke of the pen, Pa Chin summarizes the story as follows: "But he spoke in Russian. And no one understood him."[8] The bystanders may not have understood him, but there is little doubt that the reader has no difficulty in understanding the Russian's tragedy. This, of course, is the story's achievement.

III   *The Dispossessed*

In the 1920s and 1930s, the French Concession and the International Settlement in Shanghai were special areas outside the jurisdiction of Chinese courts. Businessmen, political dissenters, underworld figures, and an assortment of other social types lived there. With their own constables and courts, those who lived there, foreigners especially, were free to do as they pleased. Many conducted themselves disgracefully in public and aroused the anger of the Chinese, who felt that they had been displaced in their own country. To illustrate what it means to live in one's own country but to be treated as a sub-human is the theme in "Kou" ("Dog").

The story's narrator is also its central protagonist. He never identifies himself but says merely: "I do not know my name or my age. Like a stone that has been tossed into this world I came into existence. I do not know my father or my mother. I am merely something that was lost. I have yellow skin, dark hair and eyes, a flat nose and am short. I am one among hundreds of millions; fate placed me among them and made me live among them."[9]

During his childhood he had received no affection and had lived in hunger and cold. A kind, elderly man advised him to try to get an education. In trying, he wandered among the grand and humble structures that people call schools, but no one would admit him. This rejection fits into the pattern of his experience and makes him wonder if he is human.

At last he finds a decrepit temple in which to live; he prays and asks the idol in it if he is human. But the idol does not answer.

Unsatisfied with eating the scraps that people throw away, he continues to search for an answer to his identity. He attaches a straw price tag to his back and goes to the marketplace, offering himself for sale, but no one is interested in buying him. Like a beggar, he roams the streets and dreams of fresh food, clean clothes, and a warm house. But he tells himself that those things belong to a man.

One day he sees a pair of shapely legs walking alongside a white puppy dog. Envying the good fortune of the dog, he rushes to embrace the woman's legs. Someone seizes him, throws him to the ground, kicks him, and calls him mad. Back in the temple, he concludes that he is lower than a dog and prays to the idol: "God, please be my father, and let me become a dog, exactly like that white-haired one."[10] As usual, the idol keeps his mouth shut, unaware of the supplicant's "barking" and "crawling" on the floor.

His search for an identity continues. One evening, sitting by a wall and rubbing his muddy sore feet, he hears someone yelling, calling him a dog. He hurries back to the temple and thanks the idol for having given him an identity; he now expects to enjoy the privileges of a dog.

The next time he sees that pair of shapely legs moving down the street, he rejoices inwardly. When the woman gets closer to him, he again embraces her legs, expecting to be loved like a good dog. But someone immediately kicks him and the woman's dog bites him. When he opens his eyes, he finds himself in a dark, cold cellar and can detect no human sound. Hardly able to breathe and aching all over, he tells himself: "No matter how much it hurts me, I am after all a dog. I must bark and bite. I must bite loose the rope that ties me and return to the temple."[11]

Much of the experience in this story is externally imposed; that is, each scene, through allusive reference, is meant to carry a special meaning. Pa Chin achieves a limited success in creating occasions to accommodate his allegorical purposes. The invisible "I" is no one and, at the same time, potentially every unwanted, lowly Chinese. The idol and the temple are all he has. The former is an image of authority but a strangely silent one, and the latter is the only shelter where he can stay without being harassed. The lady, her puppy, and those with green eyes and long noses are almost literally omnipresent and omnipotent gods; the narrator's self-musings in the cellar can be interpreted symbolically to mean the Chinese's desire to continue his struggle — to find his own identity.

While "Dog" is a parable allegorizing the lowliness of the Chinese in their own country, "Wu-shih to-kuo" ("More Than Fifty") portrays the hardships and sufferings of a group of more than fifty peasants, whose villages have been destroyed by floods and whose homes have been pillaged and burned by rampaging soldiers. With few belongings, the group, made up of old and young, male and female, has been on the road for more than six months without finding any place to settle down. On the way, a widow unselfishly sells her seven-year-old son to feed the group for two days; one of the older men falls and dies shortly afterwards; the group gets lost in a forest in the midst of a winter storm; and one innocent eleven-year-old girl asks her grandmother: "Why don't we have rice to eat? ... Why don't we have a house to live in?"[12] What the girl wants is what the narrator in "Dog" wanted: the basic necessities of life. However, unlike "Dog," with its allegorical implications, "More Than Fifty" is written in a realistic, even naturalistic manner. Its merit lies in its portrait of a group of dispossessed people who are to be remembered for their simple and moving speech, their basic sympathy for one another, and their determination to survive.

IV   *The Intellectuals*

"The sun is setting with no road ahead, / In vain I weep for loss of country... / Although I die yet I still live, / Through sacrifice I have fulfilled my duty...."[13] So wrote Ch'iu Chin (1875–1907), a female revolutionary, before her execution by the Manchus in July 1907. Her tragic end dramatized the role of student revolutionaries in the revolution of 1911 and in all Chinese cultural and political movements during the first two decades of the twentieth century.

In Pa Chin's early fiction, he expressed his unbounded admiration for such intellectuals through such characters as Tu Ta-hsin, Li Leng, and others in *The Love Trilogy* who heroically sacrifice their lives for the betterment of mankind. It is, then, easy to see why Pa Chin would condemn other intellectuals whose only action is in talk and not in deeds. His description of them may remind the reader of T. S. Eliot's "hollow men": "Shape without form, shade without color, / Paralysed force, gesture without motion."[14] Just as Eliot's men do not lack eloquence, Pa Chin's hollow intellectuals, such as Professor Yüan Jun-shen in *Destruction* and Professor Li Chien-hung and the student Chang Hsiao-ch'uan in *Rain,* all use admir-

ably disciplined language; they do not protest much, except by
"leaning together," whispering together, and uttering irreproach-
able sentiments. Comfortable in their surroundings, Yüan Jun-
shen closes his small, nearsighted eyes to recall his abortive love
affair with a French girl and looks forward to his courting of Miss
Li Ching-shu; Professor Li Chien-hung frequently expresses as a
lofty ideal having the young educated go abroad before allowing
them to participate in meaningful revolutionary work; and Chang
Hsiao-ch'uan proudly sprinkles his speech with foreign words and
expressions to exhibit his erudition.

Though Pa Chin's criticism of such intellectuals is to be found
throughout his fiction, in his short story "Ch'en-lo" ("Sinking
Down") he presents a coherent picture of the hollowness of many
intellectuals. The protagonist is a Professor Anonymous, whose
views on education for the young are nearly identical with those of
Professor Li Chien-hung in *Rain*. To a student he says: "I advise
you to study more books. This is very important. Any person who
has studied little is useless. What China needs is more diligent students; China has no use for student demonstrators. And you, the
young people, don't even read. How can this be? To recover the
Northeast from the Japanese also depends on studying."[15] Furthermore, like Professor Yüan in *Destruction,* he believes in inaction or
nonresistance vis-à-vis evil, explaining: "Everything that exists has
a reason for being there, and that includes the existence of Manchukuo; evil is inevitable and it will disappear in time...."[16] As in
Eliot's "death's dream kingdom" where nothing happens and
there are no confrontations, Professor Anonymous, wearing deliberate disguises, turns his eyes away from his young wife's adulter-
ous affair with his young colleague and former student and comforts himself with the study of ancient literature and porcelain
vases.

In Eliot's poem are the following lines: "Those who have
crossed / With direct eyes to death's other Kingdom / Remember
us — if at all — not as lost / Violent souls, but only as the hollow
men / The stuffed men."[17] It seems that in "Sinking Down," the
only person who has "direct eyes" is the young narrator. He is
aware of the hollowness of Professor Anonymous's life, of the professor's spiritual stagnation, and of the professor's inability to take
any kind of action. While to others the professor's life seems to be
successful and filled with fame, social status, a young wife, a mansion, and a house full of rare Japanese, Chinese, and English

books, to the narrator it is characterized by hollowness, loneliness, darkness, and death, and the professor is an example of complete negation of the will. While the public mourns the professor's death as a great loss to Chinese culture, the young narrator views it as the final release for a man who has been living a life of lies and shadows, and he concludes: "As for me, I heaved a sigh of relief at his death and felt not the slightest sense of loss. I was even happy about it. The voice of 'nonresistance to evil' has forever died with him."[18]

Are these hollow intellectuals ever capable of action? Pa Chin thinks they are, but that when they take action it is frequently devoid of moral principles. In "Chih-shih chieh-chi" ("The Intelligentsia"), Pa Chin writes about professors intriguing against one another in a fierce battle for power. A Professor Wang, for his security and immediate gain, yields totally to the pressure of the students and his colleagues and joins them in sacking the college president, his benefactor, whom he has vowed to support.

In addition to the hollow intellectuals whom he despises, Pa Chin presents another type of intellectual in *Shen, kuei, jen (God, Ghost, Man)*. In "God," the first story in the volume, Pa Chin describes a devout Japanese Buddhist. Having shed his identity as a radical when he realized his inability to change things, he now fasts occasionally, chants sutras, and withdraws from the world as much as possible. In his passive approach to life he reads nothing, not even the newspaper, because he can find no news which does not relate to war, slaughter, catastrophe, and universal suffering. Instead, he concentrates upon becoming a seer. The second story, "Ghost," describes a Japanese schoolteacher's firm belief in the existence of a supernatural world and of ghosts. He tells the narrator: "If there are no ghosts, then where in the world can we find justice?"[19] And the last story, "Man," describes an inmate in a Tokyo police detention center and his insistence on being identified as a man and on his right to steal books written by André Gide, Friedrich Nietzsche, and Leo Tolstoy.

There is a common theme running through the three stories. Each is about an intelligent and disillusioned man searching for meaning in life. Each has developed a belief or defense mechanism which enables him to live in a world that he sees to be full of suffering, injustice, and oppression. There remains the narrator himself. Even though he mildly disapproves of the actions of the Buddhist and the schoolteacher and sympathizes with the thief in "Man," he is wise enough to envy them — those who can believe. He knows how difficult it is to retain human dignity without the support of some "illusion." But if he is too intelligent for the simple and unattractive beliefs of the Buddhist or of the schoolteacher, he is also too honest to pretend to the kind of logic advanced by the thief. In place of the Buddhist's sutra-chanting, the schoolteacher's seance sessions, and the thief's declaration of innocence, he has nothing tangible to offer except a vague sense of dissatisfaction with the status quo. This sense of dissatisfaction typifies the problems faced by Chinese intellectuals during the mid-1930s, and particularly by Pa Chin himself.

V *Fables*

In the January 1937 preface to *Ch'ang-sheng t'a* (*Pagoda of Long Life*) Pa Chin writes: "Reality has often so oppressed me that I can hardly breathe. My hands and feet are bound by invisible chains. Yet in my dreams I experience total freedom. I must not allow my dreams to be forgotten, so I shall record some of them. They are like the dreams of a child, and I arbitrarily call them fables. But in truth, they should have been more appropriately called 'dream words.' "[20] This was a period of personal crisis for Pa Chin. He had just returned from Japan and felt that he was achieving little in his life despite his fame as a writer. This dark mood was expressed through his nostalgic yearning for his past, particularly for his father, whom he wrote of fondly in the preface. Even though his father had been dead for a long time, he frequently dreamed of him, and in his dreams he relived his childhood.

Seeking to represent what he felt to be a reality of life, Pa Chin wrote four stories; in each, a father tells his child a fable. The first is "Ch'ang-sheng t'a" ("Pagoda of Long Life"); the second, "T'a ti pi-mi" ("Secret of the Pagoda"); the third, "Yin-shen chu" ("The Invisible Pearl"); and the fourth, "Neng-yen shu" ("The Talking Tree"). All of them are deceptively simple, though they deal with the complex nature of contemporary life. For the sake of his message, Pa Chin sacrifices literary fullness by telling, instead of showing, the reader. For example, "Pagoda of Long Life" begins with a one-sentence paragraph: "A long time ago there was an emperor..."[21]; "The Invisible Pearl" begins with the father telling his child: "Child, rest a little bit. I think you're a little tired."[22]

The common theme in his fables is the darkness of human existence. Both "Pagoda of Long Life" and "Secret of the Pagoda" deal with an inhumane and cannibalistic emperor and his court, which is a real slaughterhouse and reflects at its worst the world as Pa Chin saw it. "The Invisible Pearl" is concerned with the persecution of innocent country folks, the legend of a boy turning into a dragon, and the drowning of villagers. And "The Talking Tree" is about the enslavement and imprisonment of innocent young boys by a wicked emperor. In each of the stories, Pa Chin attributes human suffering to institutions which change ordinary men into conscienceless monsters. Such human monsters believe that immortality, authority, and power are more important than people.

Despite the pervading darkness, Pa Chin's overall view is not entirely without hope. The talking tree's last words to a long-suffering brother and sister are as follows: "Go away. Help others, sympathize with others, love others. Help, compassion, love — these are without sin."[23] The words are moving, not only because they affirm life, but because they are also pleas for uncritical love and compassion.

Pa Chin's choice of the fable form provides a change from his realistic portrayals of human existence. He probably believed that the reader needed a suspension of reality from time to time to go on living in a world dominated by war, slaughter, and an infinite number of daily atrocities. Lest the reader misunderstand his true intentions, Pa Chin's messages are stated overtly and without disguise, as one would expect in openly didactic fables. For Pa Chin is not really a fantasist. He fails to merge the kingdoms of magic and common sense by using words that apply to both; in fact, the mixture he has created does not come alive. His criticism of human nature is too didactic and the stories do not contain the mixture of realism, wittiness, charm, and mythology necessary for good fantasy.

VI *Stories of Love*

Pa Chin wrote not only political stories; he also wrote about the lives of ordinary people. In the prefaces to several volumes of his short stories, he repeatedly emphasized that he wanted to write about human happiness, love, hatred, and suffering.[24] These themes are best reflected in his stories of love and violence.

Through poetry, drama, fiction, and even the essay, literature has been constantly concerned with human love in its anguish and pain, its joy and comfort, and its aberrations, cruelty, and pettiness, as well as its fullness, passion, and beauty. In Pa Chin's love stories, the reader will find more anguish, pain, aberrations, cruelty, and pettiness than joy and comfort, fulfillment, passion, and beauty. The love stories can be divided into ones dealing with love between man and woman — unmarried and married — and with parental love.

In Pa Chin's first volume of short stories, *Revenge,* there is "Ch'u-lien" ("First Love"), a traditional story of unrequited love between a young Chinese student and a French girl. When it was first published in 1930, it attracted a great deal of favorable attention from a public which was then much interested in reading about foreigners and their way of life.

Apart from its interesting subject matter, "First Love" is a story told with a unified point of view and with a heavy emphasis on its hero's feelings. Briefly, a group of friends have gathered to talk about "first love," a subject that makes them forget the realities of life and enables them to live, even if temporarily, in their memories of the beautiful past. In the group is Mr. T'ang, who recalls that more than ten years ago he was a student in France. For health reasons he went to the south of France and rented a room from a kind landlady. Through the landlady and her daughter he met Marie, a teenage girl of sixteen or seventeen who was studying in a local girls' school and staying with her aunt and uncle, since her father lived in Paris, where he owned a store. Soon, T'ang and Marie fell in love. They saw each other at least once every other day, happily sharing their dreams and plans for a future together. One day Marie fails to show up at their rendezvous. Returning to his room, T'ang learns from the landlady's daughter that Marie had come to bid him good-bye because her father insisted she return to Paris and prepare for a career in the theater. Soon afterwards, T'ang becomes ill, but gradually recovers. He tries to find Marie in Paris and elsewhere, but to no avail. Marie has vanished. Now ten years later, all he has is a picture of her and his memories.

The story itself is ordinary enough, but Pa Chin has concentrated not on the story but on showing T'ang's feelings at his first and succeeding meetings with Marie and at their separation. Noteworthy, for example, is their first meeting. T'ang recalls: "I paid particular attention to her. The way she laughed was really captivating. Her entire body shook a little. Entrancing also were her small mouth that constantly opened and closed and the two rows of pearly white teeth like white jade.''[25] And after Marie has told T'ang that she would welcome his visits, T'ang again notices her "gorgeous teeth." T'ang seems to be completely overwhelmed, not by what Marie has said, but by what his transfiguring imagination has made of her. He purposefully makes her smile, and whenever she does, "'inside her tiny crimson mouth one could see her snow-white teeth glisten. That afternoon, she wore a violet dress with small floral designs of white. Around her neck was a golden locket and chain. Her neck and hands and arms were completely exposed.''[26]

In contrast, there is the pain of separation, of which T'ang says: "After returning to my room, I cried for a long time and forgot everything. I felt only my loneliness and the meaninglessness of life. Then I thought of the good times we had had together, and was able to understand why she had come to the house to say good-bye when she knew that I would be elsewhere waiting to meet her, for in this way she could spare me sorrow.''[27]

If "First Love" is rather traditional, "Lo-po-erh hsien-sheng" ("Monsieur Robert") is a love story with a twist to the ending. It is told by a young boy who gradually becomes involved with the protagonist of the story. With a boy's curiosity, he notices M. Robert, a man in his fifties with sparse and graying hair who sings a love song every evening. The lyrics include the following: "At the meadow's edge when your beautiful form appeared, / The stars gathered together their light, / The nightingale ceased its singing, / The moon, mortified, covered its face, / Ashamed to face your beauty... / I gaze vacantly at the sky, / The sky makes me think of your face, / I gaze vacantly at the sea, / The sea makes me think of your love. / But the sky, ah! is not as pure as your face, / Nor is the sea as deep as your love!...''[28]

At first the boy finds M. Robert disgusting; he feels that M. Robert sings the song badly, and that a man of his age should not be singing such sentimental lyrics. But his mother thinks differently. Pitying M. Robert's loneliness, she tells her son that M. Robert is a pitiful old man; and one night, she asks him: "Tell me, no matter what might happen in the future, no matter what you might hear about your mama, would you still love her as much as you do now? Tell me, yes or no.''[29] The boy answers yes.

Soon the boy learns the song well, and one day sings it outside M. Robert's window and is invited inside M. Robert's home. A friendship develops; and whenever M. Robert sings on the other bank of the river the boy silently sings along with him in his heart. But two days later, suddenly, M. Robert stops coming to the river-bank, and his disappearance seems to worry the boy's mother.

The boy goes to see M. Robert. Sick in bed, the old man confides in the boy and tells him his life story:

Once upon a time in a certain town there was an unknown music teacher. He was a single man ... not yet forty ... not far from his house was a flower shop which he always passed when he went to the lycée to teach music.

The proprietor of the flower shop was an old lady. She had a daughter, at that time not quite twenty, whose face wasn't beautiful but who had exceptionally beautiful eyes. Every time the music teacher passed the flower shop he would see her standing by the door.... He tried in every way to catch her fancy, talking to her of love, and often going dancing or strolling with her ... one day he tricked the girl into doing something she shouldn't have done. After that she promised to marry him even though she didn't love him....

When her mother found out about it, she was determined not to let her daughter marry the music teacher. He, however, managed to talk the girl into promising to elope with him, and prepared everything. Yet, when the time came, the girl broke her promise — perhaps her mother found out about the plan and stopped her — and the music teacher went away alone.

For some time he wandered, living here and there, but no matter where he went, he couldn't forget either the girl or his love for her.... A year later he went back to his hometown, but the girl had gone. He heard she had married someone else and had had a boy. The child was the music teacher's, of course, but only the girl and he knew it.[30]

M. Robert speaks faster and faster as if he fears that someone will stop him. In telling the story he calls the girl Marie-Paule, which is the name of the boy's mother. Quickly, the boy asks: "Marie-Paule? ... Then your son, no ... her son, isn't he four-teen this year?" The music teacher has already fallen back on his bed and could say no more. Frantically, the boy shakes the music teacher and shouts: "Tell me quickly, is he or is he not fourteen?"[31] After some time, M. Robert opens his eyes, looks at the boy, and nods.

The story is concerned more with the effect of unrequited love on M. Robert. The music teacher's confession is vital to the boy's growing up, to his discovery of his true identity, and to his aware-ness of what lies underneath the surface of his observations. Tech-nically, the surprise ending is achieved through Pa Chin's withholding one important piece of information from the reader as long as possible, so that only as the reader finishes the story does he fully understand the significance of the previous action. And the ending explains M. Robert's habit of singing his love song along the riverbank directly across from the boy's home, and the boy's mother's sympathy with the music teacher.

Similar to "Monsieur Robert" in its confessional tone is "Ai ti shih-tzu chia" ("The Cross of Love"), which is written in the epistolary form. A self-proclaimed "lazy, self-destructive and psychotic" person writes to a friend who has been his host for more than two months but can no longer tolerate him. The letter eloquently describes events which began six years earlier. Married to a girl chosen for him by his uncle, he took her to Nanking, where he had a job. A year later, he lost the job. His unemployment caused his wife much anguish. Out of a warped sense of duty, she committed suicide, thinking that her death would relieve his burdens. Sadly, he took her coffin back to her parents and stayed with them for a while. His beautiful sister-in-law offered to marry him in his late wife's stead but he firmly rejected her and began a life of penance.

In the story, the wife's example reminds the reader of many self-sacrificing heroines found in romantic fiction. Her willingness to sacrifice her life for her husband, ironically, only adds to his burdens. Furthermore, so deeply does he feel guilt and responsibility for her death, that he can no longer function in life. And despite the moral and psychological toughness achieved during these years, he still repeats to himself over and over: "My heart is dead. Everywhere I go I see that coffin, reminding me that a woman has sacrificed her life for me ... I drift, I loaf, and I drink...."[32] In short, the story tells of a dead wife, and a husband who is alone, wandering and suffering; a love that should have flourished in the sunlight had only one year of happiness to be followed by six years of darkness and probably many more filled with regret and sorrow. What matters is that in the story the color of self-sacrifice is also the color of death and eternal sorrow.

"First Love," "Monsieur Robert," and "The Cross of Love" all stress the disappointments and despair associated with romantic love, while "Hao jen" ("A Good Man") stresses marital convenience. In the story, a Chinese narrator with a highly developed sense of right and wrong is dissatisfied with the work he does and with himself. He despises the fact that all he has learned is to "flatter superiors, manage subordinates, play cards, see plays, drink wine and eat."[33] He has found it difficult to adjust the facts of his life to the morality he had been taught at school — a morality of absolute right and wrong, of beauty and truth. Every time his psychological conflicts come to the surface, he looks at a little book with a blue cover and reads the flyleaf inscription, which says: "To my young friend, Wang." And he remembers the writer's initials, C. M., and particularly C. M.'s story.

C. M. was Charles Meudon, a friend he had had in Paris. A bookseller, Meudon supplied him with the books he wanted. What struck him about Meudon was that Meudon had married a very young woman. When he knew Meudon better, he asked him about his marriage. To his question, Meudon answered simply: "What is so strange about it? I don't think it is strange at all. It is very natural — she needs me, I need her, that's all."[34] Still curious, he pressed Meudon to tell him more.

Finally Meudon tells him an engrossing story. Meudon had raised as his own daughter an abandoned girl who in time became interested in a young man. Worried that she might leave him, Meudon told the suitor that the girl wasn't really his daughter, that her father had been a prisoner in an African penal colony, her mother had drowned herself, and that her parents had never been married. As a result, the young man wrote her a letter and explained why he could not and did not want to marry someone of her background. After she received the letter, she cried and went to see him. But he rejected her. Learning that he was taking a night train to Paris one evening, she ran to the station to plead with him a last time. There was a big snowstorm that evening, and she was later found beneath a cedar tree, frozen and barely breathing. Sick for a month or two, she recovered, but lost her hearing completely. Not only was she deaf; she never had any interest in other young men. And since she already knew her true relationship to Meudon, she agreed to marry him. During their years of marriage, she had been quite happy with Meudon.

The narrator considered that Meudon had acted unethically. And even after many years, every time he looks at Meudon's gift-book to him, he wonders: "In the final analysis can he [Meudon] be counted as a good man or not?"[35] This is the moral question that appears to be of central importance in the story.

The story, Pa Chin hoped, would enrich the reader's breadth of human experience, complicate and humanize his approach to life.

It does not try to convince the reader of the validity of any particular moral concept. To the narrator, Meudon has violated the bond of human kindness and resorted to trickery to acquire his wife. What the narrator represents is the conventional view; his concept of right and wrong, learned at school, is absolute and unbendable. But Meudon believes that what he did was completely justified by his belief in a higher law or principle of human need. He simply cannot imagine any natural law or ethic which might take precedence over his need for a wife. For him, conventional human conduct is not sacred — only human need can make human acts sacred. Having arrived at this belief, he views the suitor of his "daughter" as a threat to something he needs badly; the threat naturally brings forth a strong reaction from him. What is significant is not whether Meudon is right or wrong in an absolute sense, but that he is true to his own beliefs. By insisting on his own terms, he has made the narrator rethink and reexamine his old precepts about right and wrong as well as beauty and truth. And in turn, the story makes the reader reexamine his own moral order. Here lies the strength of the story.

An entirely different type of love story is "Fu yü tzu" ("Father and Son"), which, as the title indicates, emphasizes the complex relationship between a father and his son. Divided into fifteen sections and written in simple, straightforward language devoid of flourishes, a first-person narrator tells the reader of the tension that has been building up in the years since the birth of his son, named Min, and how minor arguments between him and his wife invariably lead to her siding with the son, prompting him to see his own son as an intruder: "I myself never had a father's love. I hated him [his son] because he destroyed my happy life."[36] Tension mounts, and one night after having physically abused his son, he takes Min out of the house in a mad rage, uncertain of his next step and muttering to himself that he wants to kill him. Caught in a downpour, they take shelter under a roof-eave and he calms down.

There follows a dramatic scene in which father and son find their true selves and become reconciled with each other:

I wiped the raindrops off my forehead and tidied my hair. Under the street light I looked at the child in my arms, and I thought: I have now triumphed.

The child was obviously scared, his face pale, his head wet with raindrops, his rain-soaked hair sticking to his forehead, his small body shivering within his wet clothing. His two small hands clung tightly to my neck, and his eyes looked at me in fear.

"Good daddy, I'm wrong. I won't cry anymore; I won't cry anymore. Let's go home. It's cold here," he repeated pitifully, affectionately, and frightened.

Silently I looked at his small face, as if I didn't understand what he said. By this time, my anger had disappeared. There was no one nearby, not even a shadow — just Min and me.

"Good daddy, let's go home. Mom is waiting for us. It's cold here. I won't cry, I won't groan and moan, and I will obey you."

Continuously, pitifully, affectionately, frightfully he repeated those words. My face touched his, wet, icy cold and tiny.

I was confused, I was hesitant. I felt as if I were dreaming. I pondered awhile, not knowing what to do. Then I suddenly understood and my eyes filled with tears.

I suddenly forgot myself and began to kiss Min's tiny face. . . .[37]

VII   *Stories of Violence*

One of the best of Pa Chin's stories of violence is "Fu-ch'ou" ("Revenge"). Like the narrator in "A Good Man," who learned to reexamine his concepts of right and wrong, the narrator in "Revenge" learns not only about himself but also about the human condition in general. Structured like a web, "Revenge" begins with an unassuming narrator saying in a matter-of-fact manner: "This year I accepted my old friend Peiresc's invitation to spend the summer with him in his villa. When I arrived, there were already some guests in the villa. One was a doctor, named Laceauros; another was Flamant, a journalist; still another was called Pierton, said to be a high-school teacher. This was the first time I had met any of them."[38] He goes on to say that the villa was located in a quiet village set amid beautiful scenery with a church nearby. One evening, the guests discussed the question of happiness.

The doctor insists that revenge is the greatest happiness on earth. He says that two years previously he was staying at an inn in Italy. One night he was roused from his sleep by the proprietess of the inn and told that another guest, a young man, had committed suicide. The doctor examined the victim's body and found a letter addressed to "whoever finds my body" in one of the pockets. When he read the letter he found out that the dead man was one Faulkenstein, the assassin of General Mihanoff, and realized that he now possessed a secret that all Europe was eager to discover.

Faulkenstein's letter was a straightforward recital of his past. Years ago, he lived in a small town in south Russia and married a woman named Ida. They ran a grocery store and lived happily until one day he saw an officer hurriedly leaving his store. When he went in, he found his wife had been raped and murdered. He recognized the officer as a Lt. Matachinko and rushed to general headquarters to report the crime to General Mihanoff. The general smiled politely and detained him in prison for two days. When he was released from prison, he found his store had been looted. Having lost everything, he left home, changed his name, and became a cab driver, awaiting his chance for revenge.

One night a drunken officer whom Faulkenstein recognized as Matachinko hired his cab. He drove it to the riverbank, identified himself to his enemy, and cold-bloodedly plunged a dagger into Matachinko's chest. He pulled out the dagger and wiped the blade with his tongue until he had cleaned it of every drop of Matachinko's blood. He then threw the corpse into the river and waited patiently for an opportunity to kill General Mihanoff.

It was not to be an easy task. For years he trailed the general from Kiev to Odessa, from St. Petersburg to Geneva, and finally to Paris. He learned that the general frequented the Café Lumiere, and he stalked his enemy there. Finally his chance came. He shot the general three times and fled the scene. Having lived a life of privation and ignominy, and having accomplished his purpose in life, he felt he had no recourse but to commit suicide.

One can see from the way he narrates the story that the doctor clearly has mixed feelings about it. Though he sympathizes with Faulkenstein, he also feels that revenge is a terrible thing. At which point, the journalist interrupts: "I think you'd better give me that letter of confession to be published. This will solve the Mihanoff case. What good will it do for you to keep Faulkenstein's secret forever?"[39] The schoolteachers says nothing, but Peiresc comments: "In these days, it's an eye for an eye, and a tooth for a tooth. There is no other way."[40]

The weblike structure serves a useful purpose. In the center of the web is Faulkenstein's confession, which strikes the various members of the doctor's audience differently. To the journalist, it is a story that needs to be published; from Pierton, the schoolteacher, it evokes no response at all; to Peiresc, it reaffirms his unquestioned belief in old-fashioned justice, where man takes the law in his own hands. It seems to Pa Chin that the journalist, the schoolteacher, and the host have all missed the true significance of Faulkenstein's tale in their inability to see below the surface. But the effect on the doctor is more complicated than on the others. Emotionally, he empathizes with Faulkenstein in his declaration that "revenge" is the greatest happiness on earth; but rationally he knows that a crime is a crime.

The meaning of the story lies in the first narrator's reaction. His profession never clearly identified and his name never given, he appears to be the least worldly among the audience. And the quiet luxuries of his host's villa, the peaceful village, and the solace of the church in the distance are inadequate to protect him from the harsh realities of life. Instead of rushing to a quick conclusion about Faulkenstein, he merely raises his head and gazes "at the multitude of stars dancing in the deep blue sky."[41] The conclusion implies that human motives and human behavior are often too complex for simple generalizations and, if nothing else, they certainly make one wonder about the complexities of human experience.

"Revenge" is a successful story. Not only does it cleverly employ a weblike structure, it is also devoid of editorial comments and intrusions. In it the reader sees a happy presentation of theme through structure.

Similar in structure to "Revenge" is "Fang-tung t'ai-t'ai" ("Mrs. Landlady"). "Mrs. Landlady" has a layer-cake structure which helps Pa Chin protest against human misery, in this case the cost of war — the wounds, the deaths, the bereavements. Typical of Pa Chin's short stories, it does not begin with the landlady herself or with the events which are the chief concern of the narrator, but with a "frame" device. A Chinese student opens the story but the main narration is done by his landlady, Mme. Guillaumin.

In the first layer of the story is Mme. Guillaumin. She is a born storyteller, one impelled to relate events as if she were the voice of all human suffering. She has three stories. One is an account of what it was like during the First World War:

The war — ah, we had more than our share. In the beginning, on August 1, 1914, when France was formally mobilized, we were still behind the lines, but in less than two weeks the front lines suffered defeat after defeat and retreated, and the sense of urgency increased every day. The streets were so crowded with the comings and goings of automobiles, goods-carts, bicycles, horse-carts, and tanks that a person could hardly cross the street. It seemed as though the hubbub of horses' hoofs, the bugle calls, and the soldiers' cries would deafen everyone, and the news reports grew worse and worse. The "Boches' "* cry of "To Paris" echoed like thunder. . . .

The French army retreated and the "Boches" came. The wealthy and their valuables had long before moved to Paris in fully laden cars. . . . As soon as the "Boches" arrived, their first action was to seize whatever they could use or enjoy and plunder it. And they subjected all women, with the exception of the very old, to their abuse; they did what they pleased. . . .[42]

The second story concerns the Dellile family, which consisted of a sick father and a seventeen-year-old daughter. When the fighting erupted around them, M. Dellile ran out of the house and was shot and wounded by the "Boches." The young daughter, Denise, pleaded with the "Boches" to allow her to take her father to a doctor but they denied her request and accused M. Dellile of having been a spy. That evening, a squad of soldiers was sent to Denise's house to keep an eye on her. During an ugly brawl among the soldiers, three of them were killed and Denise wounded. Two days later, Denise's father died in a "Boches" prisoner-of-war camp, and a week after that it was reported that Denise had poisoned the drinking water of the "Boches" and then shot herself.

As the landlady continues to tell her stories to the Chinese student, a very elderly woman comes to the house and calls out: "Mme. Guillaumin, good evening. Maurice has come back! Have you seen him! ... He's the battalion commander. ... Didn't you hear the bugle? ... I must go! I want to meet him. ..."[43] This interruption is the beginning of the third tale. The landlady identifies the deranged woman as a Mme. Guerin, who had two sons, both of whom were drafted during the war and sent to the front at Verdun. The eldest son, Christophe, was killed; the other, Maurice, was taken prisoner and later escaped from the "Boches." Soon the government sent Maurice back to the front, but no one had heard from him ever since. As a result, his mother has become mentally deranged.

The last part of the story revolves around the thoughts of the Chinese narrator. Ineptly, he equates war with capitalism, both evils which enslave men. Now a factory worker at Laon, France, he draws a parallel between himself and those who went to war: "in

---

*Pa Chin's note: "This is the way the French disparage the Germans — like the Chinese cursing the foreign devils."

those places innumerable lives had already been thrown away, and
moreover, innumerable lives would continue to be thrown
away.... Yet, what son is not born of a mother? But I myself had
walked into the large bloody mouth of a factory."[44]

The stories discussed in this chapter are some of the best written
by Pa Chin before the Sino-Japanese War started in earnest in
1937. Almost everyone of them has some merit, whether it be in the
depth of character delineation, in intriguing plot development, or
in an examination of morals and ethics. Apart from their technical
excellence in one aspect or another, what makes these stories worth
reading and analyzing is their concern with man's search for meaning in life. This search is carried on by politically concerned characters as well as by those who never think of politics. The triumphs
and defeats of these people are what literature is all about; in this
sense, Pa Chin can be called a true artist, one seeking to present his
vision of man in a complex world.

CHAPTER 4

The Turbulent Stream *Trilogy*

I *Attacking the Family System*

DURING the May Fourth era Chinese youth responded enthusiastically to the ideas propagated in *New Youth* and in other progressive magazines. *New Youth,* edited by Ch'en Tu-hsiu, was so popular that its circulation reached 1.6 million copies after 1917, and many issues were reprinted several times because of public demand.[1] These magazines advocated intellectual and social reforms, stressed the importance of Western science and technology, attacked outmoded Chinese institutions, and accelerated the decline of the old family system.[2]

Prior to the revolution of 1911, the family was the most fundamental Chinese social unit. An individual was under the influence of his family from cradle to grave, particularly if he came from a large famlily with three or more generations living together under one roof. Such a family played an important role in the functioning of the traditional kinship system, and its ruling principle was the Confucian kinship canons, which stressed relations between father and son and husband and wife, rigid parental control of married sons, and the structuring of family membership according to sex and age. The system had worked well enough to be a major basis of Chinese civilization for several millennia.[3]

But the introduction of Western ideas and industrial influences changed all that. Starting at least as early as K'ang Yu-wei's (1858–1927) reform movement in 1898, and continuing with Dr. Sun Yat-sen's revolution of 1911 and the collapse of the Manchu government in 1912, the old imperial laws which "compelled conformity to the traditional family institution based on Confucian orthodoxy" ended.[4] And with the cultural revolution of which the

May Fourth Movement was a major part, the old family system was on the verge of total collapse.

Writings about the evils of the old family system poured out from many sources. They stressed a new role for women in the family and in society, sexual equality, freedom of social association between the sexes, marriage by free choice, greater freedom for the young, and a restructuring of the family institution along patterns common in the West.[5] Among literary works of this kind, none was more popular than Pa Chin's *Chia (Family)*, the first of the *Chi-liu (Turbulent Stream)* trilogy, which deals with the decline of the Chinese family system and particularly of the large extended family.

Pa Chin's purpose was to expose the evils associated with the traditional family system and to rescue from the "jaws of hell these victims who have lost their youth."[6] He had his eldest brother in mind as a foremost victim of the system. When he solicited his brother's opinion on the writing of the book, his brother replied: "In reality, our family system can represent all family histories. After I read *La Jeunesse* [*New Youth*] and other magazines, I longed to write such a story, but I was unable to do so. Now that you wish to attempt one, I feel elated. And I hope you have enough time to bring it to completion...."[7] By the time Pa Chin finished the sixth chapter of *Family,* entitled "Eldest Brother," he received news that his eldest brother had committed suicide. It was a crushing blow. Notwithstanding their ideological differences, he had loved his unselfish brother deeply. He completed *Family* in 1931, and its sequels, *Ch'un (Spring)*, in 1938, and *Ch'iu (Autumn)*, in 1940.

Family centers on the decline from 1919 to about 1923 of the rich Kao family of Chengtu and the rebellion of its younger members. The head of the family is called Yeh-yeh (Grandfather) or Master Kao. A widower, he lives with his concubine, Mistress Ch'en. He has three sons — Ke-ming, Ke-an, and Ke-ting; many grandchildren — including Chüeh-hsin, Chüeh-min, and Chüeh-hui, the children of his deceased eldest son; and one great-grandchild. Master Kao is a despot. A traditionalist, he believes he has the right, sanctioned by tradition, to dictate to and impose his will upon the others. As the result of this stubbornness, he and his sons cause many of the younger members to suffer and even die. On the other hand, the Kao grandchildren, represented by the three Kao brothers, are rebellious. Chüeh-hsin is a sensitive, suffering weakling; Chüeh-min is a compromiser; and Chüeh-hui is a rebel who has often been identified as the young Pa Chin himself and called "a typical figure of the young generation of the day."[8] A number of deaths occur in the novel — those of Master Kao and, in childbirth, of Chüeh-hsin's wife, and of the suicide of Ming-feng, a bondmaid. The novel ends with Chüeh-hui's forsaking the compound to go to Shanghai.

Family's immediate sequel is *Spring*. In great detail, Pa Chin describes the changes in the Kao family that occur after Grandfather's death. Ke-ming, the third-eldest son, has become the head of the family but has great difficulty in controlling his younger brothers. They defy his authority by beating up the servants, keeping concubines, and squandering the family fortune. In addition, Chüeh-hsin feels responsible for the death of his wife and his infant son (which took place in *Family*), and drinks to forget his sorrow; Chüeh-min continues his love affair with Ch'in, a modern girl, and his student activities. The novel ends with Ke-ming's daughter, Miss Kao Shu-ying, fleeing to Shanghai and declaring, "Spring is ours."[9]

In both *Spring* and *Autumn,* there is a double plot involving a family named Chou, which is related to the Kaos through the stepmother of the Kao grandsons. She was a Chou. The Chou family is a miniature Kao family, the head of which is Chou Po-t'ao, a Confucian prig who mistreats and abuses his children as his warped sense of proper Confucian conduct dictates.

In *Autumn,* the fortunes of the Kao family reach bottom. Ke-ming has lost all control over the family. His own daughter had fled to Shanghai in *Spring;* his younger brothers have become even more reckless in their behavior; his sisters-in-law more vicious in their domestic squabbling; his nieces and nephews totally undisciplined. As time goes on, deaths in the family continue, the saddest being the suicide of fifteen-year-old Shu-chen, and the death of a servant called Ch'ien-erh. On the other hand, changes have come to the Kao grandsons. Chüeh-hsin becomes more assertive. He forces Chou Hui's husband to give his cousin Hui a decent burial, and later marries a reliable woman. Chüeh-min, no longer taking any abuse from his elders, castigates them without reservation and looks forward to marrying Miss Ch'in. Shu-hua, the sister of Chüeh-hsin, Chüeh-min, and Chüeh-hui, is now openly defiant toward her uncles and aunts and has little love for the extended family.

The climax of the novel is the sale of the Kao family compound, which takes place shortly after Ke-ming's death. After the sale, the Kao grandsons and their sister live on a quiet street with their stepmother; their fourth uncle, Ke-an, keeps two households, one for his wife and the other for his lover, a homosexual opera singer; and their fifth uncle, Ke-ting, keeps two mistresses and later becomes an opium addict.

Of the three novels in the trilogy, *Family* is the most widely known. However, all three were well received by the readers of the 1930s and 1940s.[10] Apart from its timely subject matter, the popularity of the trilogy may be attributed to Pa Chin's faithful representation of reality, the exploration of the theme of the family versus the individual, and his blatant appeal to the reader's emotions.

II   *Representation of Reality*

Like the *Hung Lou Meng* (*Dream of the Red Chamber*), one of the achievements of the trilogy is its diurnal realism — Pa Chin's ability to record the daily life of both the old and young members of a traditional family during the years 1919 to 1923. He describes the lives of the elders — the dinner parties, the relationships with homosexual actors, the women's gossip and intramural bickering, the Ma-Jongg games, and the abuse of both children and servants. He is also interested in the younger family members — their rebellion against the elders, their reception of new ideas from Peking and Shanghai after the May Fourth Movement, their discussion of women's rights, and their participation in student demonstrations and in student drama productions. Besides the humdrum happenings within a large family, the novels also contain descriptions of social unrest and political agitation.

But to a reader of today, Pa Chin's description of family festivities and family gatherings are of particular interest because of his ability to capture accurately the feeling of a moment in time and space. An example is his description of the Kao family's preparation for the coming of the lunar New Year:

The traditional New Year holiday was approaching, the first big event of the year, ... and everyone was enthusiastically looking forward to it, except those who owed heavy debts which traditionally had to be repaid before the end of the year. The year's end slowly drew near, with each day bringing a new harbinger of its coming. The whole city bubbled with life. More people than usual were on the streets. Many lanterns, toys, and fire-crackers appeared. Everywhere the sound of festive horns could be heard.

...The servants, of course, were as busy as their masters, impatiently awaiting holiday festivities and the traditional gifts of cash that came their way each New Year. Every evening, the cook bustled about the kitchen making glutinous rice dumplings. During the day, the females of the family — young and old — gathered in the room of the Venerable Master [Grandfather] and folded gold and silver paper into the shape of ingots, to be burned at memorial services and thus "sent" to ancestors for their use in the next world; the women also cut intricate pictures and designs out of red and green paper — these were to be pasted on the paper windows or on oil-lamp cups.... Large red lanterns were hung in the main hall; on each of the side walls were placed panels of embroidered red silk. Ancestors' portraits were taken out of the chests in which they had been resting, and carefully hung on the hall's middle wall, there to enjoy the respects that would be paid them during the New Year Festival.[11]

On New Year's Eve, a feast is prepared:

...Eating utensils had been neatly laid on two large round tables placed in the center of the hall. The chopsticks were of ivory; the bowls, spoons and plates were silver. Beneath each plate was a red slip of paper on which a place name had been written. Three servants waited on each table: two to pour the wine, one to serve the food.... After eight varieties of coldcuts and two plates of melon seeds and almonds had been set upon the tables, members of the family, young and old, gathered in the hall. The Venerable Master Kao said "Please," and then he led everyone to sit down at their assigned seats.[12]

Matching the detailed realism of the above is the description of Master's Kao's death and the subsequent funeral arrangements:

News of a death spreads more quickly than any other. In a matter of min-utes, the whole compound knew that the old man had passed away; and a few servants were dispatched to notify the relatives of the sad news. Soon guests began to arrive. Women guests added volume to the weeping, be-wailing their own unhappy fate at the same time.

Then the work commenced. A division of labor was made between the men and the women. Three or four women relatives were assigned to sit by the body and weep. The old man was laid out on the bed and its canopy had been removed....

The Taoist priest who was to "open the road" to the next world arrived.

By divination, he decided on the propitious hour and minute for encoffin-
ing the body. The old man was bathed and dressed in his burial clothes,
then laid comfortably in the coffin with all his favorite things in life. The
coffin was stuffed full.... A troupe of Buddhist monks was next called
in. Each of these one hundred and eight monks carried a stick of lighted
incense, chanting sutras, and going in and out of the room and the courtyard.... Time for the sealing of the coffin arrived and that was ten
o'clock the next morning, a time divined by the Taoist priest. At that time
weeping reached its height, and a few mourners were shedding genuine
tears....
     All in all the Venerable Master was dead. His death brought everything
in the family to a stop. The family hall became a funeral parlor, hung with
mourning bunting; the main hall became a temple of prayer. Women wept
in the funeral parlor; monks intoned prayers in the temple. The funeral
parlor was hung with eulogy scrolls and odes to the departed; in the temple
were Buddhist idols and ten scenes from the Palace of the Afterworld....
Three days later, the mourning period officially commenced. Innumerable
gifts came pouring in, dozens of ceremonies were conducted, droves of
condolence callers arrived.... Whenever a visitor kowtowed to the spirit
of the departed, the children and grandchildren were required to do the
same, while a Master of Ceremonies intoned, "Thanks from the Filial
Sons and Grandsons." Then all would rise to their feet....[13]

III   *The Family Versus the Individual*

     The extended family is one of the oldest institutions in China,
but to Pa Chin and many others, it had outlived its usefulness and
had become a breeding ground of tyrants, parasites, and victims.
To dramatize the evils of the extended family, he relied primarily on
exposing the lives of the members of two families: the Kao family
and the Chou family. These people belong, essentially, to three
categories: defenders of the status quo, victims of the status quo,
and those who rebel against the status quo.
     The primary battleground is the Kao family compound. From
the outside it resembles other similar compounds on a quiet street
in Chengtu. A pair of crouching stone lions flank its entrance, two
big red lanterns hang from the eaves of its gate, and two large rec-
tangular stone urns stand in front of the gate. On either side of the
entrance, hung vertically on the walls, are two red veneered plaques
inscribed with black ideographs, one of which reads: "Benevolent
ruler, happy family"; and the other: "Long life, good harvests."[14]
Immediately within is the gatehouse; the main building has

sleeping-quarter wings; to the left and right are a series of court-yards and a spacious garden.

The Kao family, with its huge compound and many servants, is supported by land rented to farmers. The compound offers the family a good life. The men do not have to work but are comfortably provided for; the women need only amuse themselves with Mah-Jongg games and gossip — as long as they heed the necessities of "propriety," at least in front of the head of the compound, Master Kao. Propriety, loosely interpreted, means absolute subservience to the will of the elders, the preservation of honor, and adherence to the principles of "three obediences and four virtues."[15]

The fiercest defender of the status quo is Master Kao. Life has richly rewarded him: a handsome compound, servants, sons and grandsons, and even one great-grandson, all living "happily" under one roof. He is the epitome of a successful son who has been worthy of his ancestors, and it is his duty to perpetuate the Kao family line as long as possible, and to see that it continues to prosper. But times are changing; the world outside his compound threatens the very existence of his mode of life. What little he has heard displeases him and evokes strong negative responses from him. In a desperate effort to hold on to the past, he condemns all student activities as improper and riotous, and coeducational schooling as unbecoming for young ladies, and advocates strict adherence to the old values and virtuef.

In *Family* his misdeeds range from preventing his grandson Chüeh-hui from participating in student activities to arranging a marriage for his grandson Chüeh-min and giving the two bond-maids, Ming-feng and Wang-erh, to his friend Feng Lo-shan as concubines. His misdeeds are serious enough, particularly when one considers that he sends Wang-erh to his friend Feng as a concubine right after Ming-feng had refused to comply with his wish and committed suicide. Master Kao's insensitivity is a part of the feudal past which considers bondmaids as property of the master, to be disposed of at his will. Master Kao might even have interpreted sending Wang-erh to his friend as his way of demonstrating the power of the master, of counteracting the frighteningly progressive trends of his time. In short, Master Kao is what he is — a product of the feudal past. He is just as much a victim of the past as are those whom he victimizes.

Despite his heroic efforts to keep the family together, Master

Kao dies bitterly disappointed. As he lies on his deathbed, "he seemed to see many forms and faces drifting before him. Not one of them looked at him with any affection. There were his sons, indulging themselves in women and wine, sneering at him, cursing him behind his back. There were his grandsons, proudly going their own road, abandoning him...."[16] Pa Chin's attitude toward Master Kao is sympathetic. He might have been an entirely different sort of person under a different set of circumstances. Despite all the evils that he might have committed, at least he has conviction enough to defend the status quo in which he believes. One may fault his judgment, but never his sincerity.

No such sympathy is extended to Chou Po-t'ao, the head of the Chou family. He shares certain surface similarities with Master Kao. He too believes that the times have changed for the worse, for as he says: "The emperor is no longer like an emperor; the official not like an official; the father not like a father...."[17] What interests him is the form rather than the substance of anything. Trying to behave like a "proper" father, he insists on his daughter Hui marrying an insensitive and self-righteous man who is indirectly responsible for her early death. And after her death, Chou seems to be totally unmoved by the tragedy and implies that it was all her fault. Having learned nothing from his daughter's tragedy, he goes on to marry his seventeen-year-old son to a twenty-one-year-old woman and subjects him to all kinds of physical and mental abuse. And when the son becomes critically ill, Chou refuses to get proper medical care until the son is beyond help and dies. Chou's sin is his total disregard for the interests of his children; and in his fanatical attempts to satisfy his warped sense of proper Confucian conduct, he sacrifices the lives of both his children.

If the family is a breeding ground for tyrants, it is also a hotbed of parasites. The parasites have nothing to do other than to preserve their own interests and to compete for additional power within the family. In the trilogy, there are many parasites, among them Mistress Ch'en, the three grown sons of Master Kao, and their wives. Not only are they nonproductive members of society, they are also superstitious, hypocritical, and cruel. For instance, when Master Kao's health fails to respond to traditional medication, Mistress Ch'en hires several Taoist monks to beat drums and cymbals in the Kao's main hall and to chant prayers. She dresses herself formally in a pink shirt, kneels before a pair of candles, and mumbles prayers before an incense burner. Night after night, time after time, she rises from and falls to her knees. But as Master Kao's condition deteriorates, his three sons offer themselves as sacrifices, the idea being that they be allowed to die in their father's place. In a ludicrous ceremony, they kneel and kowtow repeatedly, though just hours before one was with his favorite female impersonator, and another was gambling and drinking in his love nest. The pace of this ludicrous show accelerates as Master Kao's condition becomes worse. One evening, Ke-ming orders that the doors of the compound be closed, "converts" it into a temple, and hires a witch doctor to chase away the evil spirits that have infested the compound. The witch doctor utters shrill cries, scatters resin, runs about the courtyard, and makes all sorts of frightening noises which, had they had any effect, would have hastened Master Kao's death. This ridiculous proceeding is halted only after Grandfather dies.

The parasites can also be cruel. After the death of Master Kao, Mistress Ch'en speaks to Ke-ming, now the head of the family, about Jui-chüeh, Chüeh-hsin's pregnant wife. Ch'en says that the "glow of blood emitted by the mother would attack the corpse and cause it to spurt large quantities of blood,"[18] and that therefore Jui-chüeh must not only leave the compound but must also move outside the city, to keep the "blood-glow" from returning to attack the body of the deceased Master Kao. This nonsensical proposal quickly gains the support of nearly all the womenfolk in the compound. Together they force Chüeh-hsin to agree to such an agreement, the end result being the death of Jui-chüeh in childbirth.

What differentiates the parasites from Master Kao is that the parasites lack the sincerity and conviction of Master Kao, for they are essentially selfish and self-serving. Whereas Master Kao deserves a degree of sympathy, the parasites deserve nothing better than utter contempt. Pa Chin's indictment of them is spoken by Chüeh-min. Arguing with his uncles about the sale of the family compound, Chüeh-min lashes out at them mercilessly:

"You think I don't know what's going on in your minds. I know everything about you. Who doesn't know about your disgusting affairs — seducing women and manhandling servants? Keeping prostitutes, lusting after female impersonators, smoking opium — which of these don't you do? Yet you have the nerve to assume the air of correct gentlemen in front of me. Why did Shu-chen jump into the well? You, the father, what were you doing at the time? Not only didn't you figure out a way to save her, but you just ran to your concubine. I've never seen such a heartless person! Your mouths are full of words about propriety and you scold others for having no respect for elders. You yourselves are offenders against propriety. You drove Grandfather to death with your vexations and you badgered Third Uncle to death. Even when Third Uncle was ill, you bothered him about selling the compound and said that he wanted the family authority for himself. All of these things you have done.... I'm not like you. I'll depend on myself to earn enough money to make a living...."[19]

Nonetheless, the parasites are an intrinsic part of the system. A monolithic force, they have the power to cause suffering and death to many.

And there are many victims of the system. They include the servants, women and meek children of harsh masters, husbands and parents. Ignorant, uneducated, and unprotected by law, they accept their suffering as part of their fate and hope that their next life may be better. Among the victims none suffers more than Chüeh-hsin, the eldest of the three Kao grandchildren. The family has deprived him of his education and his career. After his graduation from high school, though he has planned to study in Shanghai and then abroad, his father arranges a marriage for him with a woman about whom he knows little. Meek in nature, he gives up his educational plans and his childhood sweetheart, Cousin Mei, to be a good Confucian son. Later, his father arranges for him to work in a firm for a meager salary, and before he dies, his father commands him to care for his stepmother and his younger brothers and sisters.

Had Chüeh-hsin been a man without a soul, he would not have felt that the family system had cheated him. But he is a deeply sensitive man with a full knowledge of what he has been denied. He resents spending most of his time in maintaining a more or less smooth relationship with his relatives who live in the compound; he has a hard time forgetting his Cousin Mei who, after his marriage, married someone else, and was widowed and is slowly dying of tuberculosis. Aware of what he could have been, he bemoans his dreary existence. In frustration he plays mournful tunes on his bamboo flute at night and smashes the windows of the sedan-chairs.

Despite his inner discord, the system has so totally emasculated him that he has become a man whose main care is to maintain peace in the family. When his grandfather plans to arrange a marriage for his brother Chüeh-min, he agrees in principle and seeks the cooperation of his brother. Another example of his total emasculation by the system is his acceptance of the family decision to send his pregnant wife away, as a consequence of which she dies in childbirth. Granted that he is meek by nature, he is nonetheless also a victim of the system. For as the eldest son in a traditional family, his prescribed role is defined in *The Hsiao Ching* (*The Book of Filial Piety*): "The Master said: 'In serving his parents a filial son renders utmost reverence to them while at home; he supports them with joy; he gives them tender care in sickness; he grieves at their death; he sacrifices to them with solemnity. If he has measured up to these five, then he is truly capable of serving his parents.' "[20]

For Chüeh-hsin and for others like him, Pa Chin suggests that the solution lies in active rebellion. As Pa Chin's spokesman, Chüeh-hui sees the injustice of the Confucian code, which imposes filial piety on children without granting them any rights, and views patriarchy as the basis of despotism and a method by which the old control the young. He abhors the quarrels and the wrangles for power among his relatives, the clicking of Mah-Jongg tiles, the vicious gossip, the open adulteries — all fare of an ordinary day in the compound. Believing that things can be changed, he says that people should be like the peonies, "standing out in the icy breeze, never shivering a bit,"[21] and that "circumstances are man-made to begin with, and man must struggle against them constantly. It's only by conquering our environment that we can win happiness for ourselves."[22]

Putting his thoughts into action, he violates the family code by falling in love with Ming-feng, a bondmaid, becomes actively involved in student activities such as establishing a radical magazine, and participates in other work considered improper by his grandfather and illegal by the authorities. He assists his second brother, Chüeh-min, in resisting their grandfather's command that Chüeh-min marry someone whom the grandfather has chosen. His greatest moment of triumph is in the following scene, in which he condemns Mistress Ch'en and his uncles for their stupid devil-eradication campaign:

"What exactly do you think you're doing?" he asked contemptuously. He swept their faces with hate-filled eyes.

The question stopped them, cold. Ke-ming muttered something about

"driving out devils" in a tone that indicated plainly that he had no faith
whatsoever in what he was saying.
"We're eradicating devils for your grandfather," said Mistress Ch'en,
reeking of perfume and holding herself very erect. She indicated to the
witch doctor that he should enter [Chüeh-hui's room].
"You're out of your mind!" Chüeh-hui virtually spat the words in her
face. "You're not chasing devils, you're hurrying Grandfather to his
grave. You're afraid his illness won't kill him soon enough, so you're trying to exasperate him to death, scare him to death!"[23]

Soon he leaves the family and goes to Shanghai to start a new
career.
Pa Chin's message is clear. There cannot be any compromise
between the demands of the old family system and the assertion of
individual rights; the system must be destroyed. Meanwhile the
salvation of the young lies in resisting unreasonable elders, for
"every young man has the right to live, to seek freedom, knowledge, and happiness."[24] It is only through active resistance that the
young can be free, as Kao Shu-ying declares when, after fleeing her
home, she arrives in Shanghai: "Spring has come again. . . . I am
now free. Everything before me is different; everything in the past
was like a nightmare. . . . Spring belongs to us."[25]

IV *Sentimentality*

Sentimentality in literature, defined by Brooks and Warren as
"emotional response in excess of the occasion" or a "false
heightening of the pathos of the scene,"[26] was dominant in such
eighteenth-century writings as Richard Steele's *The Conscious
Lovers,* Joseph Warton's *The Enthusiast,* the poems of William
Collins and Thomas Gray, Laurence Sterne's *A Sentimental
Journey,* and Oliver Goldsmith's *The Deserted Village.* It is also a
characteristic feature of Chinese poetry about nature, time, nostalgia, and love, as well as of such traditional novels as the *Dream of
the Red Chamber, The Golden Lotus,* and other "yen-ch'ing"
(narrating-emotion) stories.
    While sentimentality by and large invokes jeers rather than tears
in twentieth-century Western writing, it occupied a preeminent
position in twentieth-century Chinese literature. One observer
noted with humor that "the modern Chinese poets were six times
more emotional than their Western colleagues because 'in the cur-
rent vernacular poetry in China there appears, on the average, one

exclamation mark in every four lines or 232 exclamation marks in every thousand lines, whereas acknowledged good poetry in foreign countries averages about one exclamation mark in every 25 lines.' "[27] Even though Hu Shih, the spokesman for the May Fourth Movement, warned against emotional excesses in literature and suggested that writers should not say they are sick or sad when, in fact, they do not feel sick or sad, modern Chinese authors such as Yü Ta-fu, Kuo Mo-jo, and Hsü Chih-mo bared their souls in confessions, diaries, and love letters.

Why did these writers choose to be so emotional? It was partly due to the influence of the bleeding-heart theory, as advanced by the Byronic Hero, upon modern Chinese literature, and partly because most writers lacked practical experience and consequently chose to emphasize feelings over action. But most important of all, their emotional works were a recognition that Chinese readers throughout history had been used to reading sentimental plays, fiction, and poetry.

Such sentimentalism can also be found in the Chinese critical vocabulary. Lin Yutang (1895–1976) tentatively singled out the following words of human emotions and feelings: "yi" (mood, inclination, intention); "ch'ing" (sentimental, passion, love, sympathy, friendly feeling); "ch'ang" (intestines, feelings, emotions); "hsing" (inspiration, happy mood, enthusiasm to do something); "ch'ü" (interesting, having flavor, the quality of being interesting to look at); "ssu" (thought, longing, idea); "mu" (loving admiration, longing from a distance); "yüan" (fretting, complaining, hating); "lien" (pity, tender love, love for what is small and beautiful); "hen" (regret, exasperation, hating the beloved); "hsi" (be tender, be careful in spending, be worried lest something is spoiled or gone).[28]

Of interest is the emphasis on *jen-ch'ing* or human sentiments. A man lacking in human sentiment is described as *"pu-chin jen-ch'ing"* or "having departed from human nature or human sentiment." A piece of writing is expected to have not only beauty of language but also beauty of sentiment, which is achieved through "intestines broken" incidents and episodes, through the successful evocation of the feelings of *mu, yüan, hen,* and *hsi.*

Modern Chinese writers forsook the traditional themes of loyalty, filial piety, chastity, and righteousness (*chung, hsiao, chieh, yi*), and stressed social themes, particularly that of love. From a survey conducted by Mao Tun covering a three-month period in 1921, it appears that more than 70 out of 115 literary works were mainly on love between the sexes.[29] In other words, writers shifted their emphasis from one subject area to another but reaffirmed the role of human emotions in their writing. Kuo Mo-jo said: "We know the essence of literature begins and ends with emotions. The aim of a literary man in expressing his emotions — whether consciously or unconsciously — always lies in eliciting the same emotional response from the readers. Thus the stronger and more pervasive the author's emotions, the stronger and more pervasive the effect of his work. This kind of work is certainly the best work."[30]

Sensitive in his feelings from childhood, it was natural that Pa Chin's writing should be extremely sentimental. Nurtured by a sentimental mother, he developed emotional attachments to everything he came in contact with. During his childhood in Kuang-yüan, he grieved at the death of a speckled hen which had been slaughtered for a feast; he mourned the death of a woman servant, Yang Sao, almost to excess; and he pleaded for the accused who were tried and tortured in his father's court. Later in Chengtu, he listened to the servants' troubles with utmost sympathy; and he watched with indignation the constant bickering among his relatives in the compound, and the physical punishment and public humiliation administered to his cousins, to the servants, and to others by his grandfather and by other elders.

His own sensitive nature explains in part why Pa Chin is noted for sentimentality in his works. To achieve this emotional effect, he creates male and female characters who too are extremely sentimental. One of their common characteristics is their romantic nostalgia. Consider, for example, Chüeh-hsin. To his boyhood girl friend Mei, he says: "Do you remember as children how we used to roll on this lawn? When an insect bit my hand, you sucked the bad blood out. We used to chase butterflies here and dye our fingernails with the juice of red balsam flowers.... Once when there was an eclipse of the moon, we took a bench and sat in the garden.... Remember? ... And those days when you studied together with us at our house. How happy we were then...."[31] Similarly, Mei dwells on her past.: "I live almost entirely on my memories now.... Memories sometimes can make you forget everything. I'd love to return to those carefree days. Unfortunately, time cannot flow backwards."[32] The past, then, seems to represent much of the innocence of perfection.

A second characteristic among Pa Chin's sentimental characters is their desire for a close identification with nature. The following is a description of Chüeh-hsin amidst the splendors of nature: "He stood a while beneath a magnolia tree, feeling rather silly, as if longing for something he knew he couldn't attain, though it was right in front of his eyes. Life seemed empty, futile. Leaning against the tree trunk, he gazed at the greenery stretching before him." [33] Similarly, no longer imbued with the vitality of nature, Mei compares herself to a dying butterfly, and nature sadly reminds her of misfortunes: "I see fading flowers and I weep. The waning moon hurts my heart. Everything recalls unhappy memories. . . . There's a tree outside my window that I planted when I went away to be married. It was budding then, but by the time I returned its branches were bare. I often think — the tree symbolizes me. . . ." [34]

In an attempt to reach his reader emotionally, Pa Chin dwells on sad occasions, and most of his characters, male or female, respond to crucial events or incidents with heartrending sobs. Often the amount of weeping a character does is directly proportionate to the degree to which he or she is victimized. Chüeh-hsin is a good example. In many ways, he has suffered more at the hands of the patriarchy than any other character; in turn he seems to weep more than anyone else. A typical example is as follows: "Tears ran down Chüeh-hsin's face as he told his story, and he was more and more wracked with sobs. Finally, unable to go on, he lay his head on the desk and wept unrestrainedly." [35]

Much of this shedding of tears is the result of such events as partings and death. Departures in *Family* bring forth an abundance of emotional feelings. Understandably, Chüeh-hui's departure for Shanghai represents a major loss to Chüeh-hsin, who tearfully tells his younger brother: "Don't forget to write along the way. I'll send you your books when you reach Shanghai. . . ." [36] And when Mei is ready to return to her mother after a short visit at the Kao compound, Chüeh-hsin feels guilty and remorseful and says to her: "You may be leaving tomorrow. We may never have a chance to see each other again, living or dead. We seem to be in two different worlds. Can you really walk off from me like this without a word of farewell?" [37]

Death plays a very significant part in the trilogy, an event which is sure to engender deep grief. Their remembrance of a deceased parent serves to unite the young Kao grandsons momentarily in a reaction of grief and loneliness. Chüeh-hsin recounts for his brothers their father's dying words and wishes. As each brother remembers his father, he is choked with a renewed sense of loss: "Chüeh-hui could no longer restrain his tears, but an instant later he stopped himself. What's past is dead and buried, he thought. Why dig it all up again now? Yet he couldn't help grieving for his departed father."[38]

Death means even more to Pa Chin's female characters. They are trapped in barren lives of emptiness and despair. Mei refers to herself often as a "dying butterfly" and dies of tuberculosis; Ming-feng drowns herself. Their deaths are a commentary on the conditions of their lives, but more importantly, they are used to arouse the reader's emotional empathy. The following is Mei's death scene, with Chüeh-hsin coming to her deathbed:

He walked to her bedside. She was lying peacefully with her eyes slightly shut, and her hair spreading upon the pillow. Her thin face was white, . . . her lips slightly parted, as if she had been about to speak when she died. Her lips were reddish and bloodish, as if the remains of blood had not been entirely wiped clean. A thin coverlet covered her body from the waist down. "I have come to see you, Mei," he said in a low voice. Suddenly he was blinded by tears and his heart was aching. "Is this how we part forever?" he wondered. "You've gone without a word. Why didn't I come earlier? Had I come sooner, I would have seen your lips quiver, heard your voice and known what you had been thinking. . . . "[39]

A scene intended to have even greater emotional impact is Pa Chin's description of Ming-feng's thoughts prior to her suicide:

When Ming-feng left Chüeh-hui's room she knew that this time all hope was gone. She did not resent him; she loved him even more. She was sure he loved her as much as ever; her lips were still warm with his kiss, her hands still felt his clasp. . . . In the long years ahead there would only be endless pain and misery. Why should she cling to a life like that? She made up her mind.

. . . She went directly to the garden, groping her way through the darkness with a great effort until she reached her objective — the edge of the lake. The waters darkly glistened; at times feeding fish broke the placid surface. She stood dully remembering many things of the past. . . . She recalled everything she and Chüeh-hui had ever said and done together. She could see every familiar tree and shrub — so dear, so lovely — knowing that she was going to leave them all. . . .

. . . She remained seated on the ground, her eyes longingly roving over the familiar surroundings in the dark. She was still thinking of him. A mournful smile flitted across her face and her eyes dimmed with tears.

Finally, she could not bear to think any longer. Rising tottering to her feet, she cried in a voice laden with tenderness and sorrow, "Chüeh-hui, Chüeh-hui" — and she plunged into the lake.[40]

Another scene meant to be heartrending is Jui-chüeh's death. Attended by a midwife, she is in a poorly furnished hut outside the city. Her husband Chüeh-hsin is not allowed into the delivery room and can only bang on the door and listen to her shrieks of pain. The following is the scene:

"Jui, I'm here, I'm here! Jui, I'm coming. Open the door. Let me in! She needs me! You let me in!" he yelled loudly, beating a wild tattoo on the door with his fists.

"Hsin, where are you? Why can't I see you? . . . it hurts! Where are you? Why don't you let him in?"

"Jui, I'm here! I will come in, I will stay by you! I won't leave you. . . . Let me in! You let me in! . . ." He screamed while beating against the door madly. . . .

Then the cries in the room stopped. A dead silence followed. That awful stillness was suddenly pierced by the bright clear wail of a new-born babe. . . . Chüeh-hsin knew that disaster had struck. . . . He went on beating against the door. . . . The door stood implacable. It wouldn't let him rescue her or even let him see her for the last time. It cut off all hope. . . .

"Jui, I'm calling you. Can you hear me?" An insane shout, embodying all his love, was wrenched from the depths of his heart. . . . But death had come.[41]

Still another scene of moving sentimentality occurs after Shu-chen's death in *Autumn*. As Chüeh-hsin and Chüeh-min bear Shu-chen's corpse in their arms on the slow journey back to her room, the scene is described in some detail:

. . . The light of the wind-and-rain lamp happened to fall on that pretty face with its small eyes and small mouth. As before it was a face which had endured and still showed misery and grief. Her bangs were pasted on her forehead. Her eyes were closed. On her left eyebrow and on her right temple there were still traces of blood. Drops of blood and water dripped down unceasingly from her hair. Her mouth was closed and at the corners there were traces of blood. Her clothes were drenched around her slight little body. But on her small feet there was left only one flower-embroidered silk slipper. One disordered pigtail hung down heavily, dripping water all the way.[42]

As the two brothers carry Shu-chen's body, Pa Chin writes: "Shu-chen's body became even heavier in their arms. This was a labor of love. This was also a painful task. This limp and slight body suddenly became like a piece of iron. Not only did it weigh heavily in their arms, but it also weighed down like a great stone in their hearts."[43]

V *Evaluation*

Like *The Golden Lotus* and *Dream of the Red Chamber,* the *Turbulent Stream* trilogy is devoted to tracing the fortunes of a modern Chinese family during a transitional period in Chinese history when old and new values clash and come into conflict. However, unlike the other two works, the trilogy is more unified in its theme and devoid of their digressions. Not only is it a faithful representation of daily life in a large Chinese family, it treats comprehensively such related themes as frustrated young love, the low status of women, concubinage, enmity between parents and children, and harsh treatment of the young — all directly attributable to the extended family system. Pa Chin attacks the system through the mouths and lives of defenders and victims of the rebels against the status quo, letting them unwittingly reveal the evil, the suffering, and the necessity for reform. Few Chinese readers can be unmoved by his intense moral fervor or his humanitarian zeal on behalf of good, kind, generous souls like Chüeh-hism who are badgered and tyrannized by selfish, hypocritical individuals and by that soulless institution — the family. In the trilogy the eternal war between right and wrong is waged not on the level of abstract moral principles but on a living stage, peopled by characters who seem real, for the moment, in spite of being exaggerated. Lastly, by appealing blatantly to the reader's emotions, Pa Chin satisfies the needs of many readers for what Aristotle called a catharsis of feeling.

CHAPTER 5

Works of the War Years

I *Introduction*

STARTING with the 1868 Meiji Restoration, Japan had consistently expanded her interest in China. In 1905, she won the Russo-Japanese War in Manchuria; during World War I she claimed the German parts of Shantung province as one of the allies (as early as 1915 she had presented her Twenty-one Demands to China and had seized Shantung); in 1931 her Kwantung army struck at Mukden, Manchuria, thus eliminating an uncertainty about her aims in China. And in early 1932 she formed the independent state of Manchukuo and installed Henry P'u Yi (1906–1967) as the puppet emperor.[1]

Despite Japan's expansion in China, Chiang Kai-shek was hesitant to wage war against a better-armed foe without having first strengthened a China that had been weakened by many years of foreign and domestic wars. Instead, he sought internal unity and the prevention of a full-scale war with Japan. But his efforts were futile, and might even have been an added incentive for Japan to exploit China's weakness and solidify her position in China.

Alarmed at the situation, Chinese writers, many of whom had left-wing sympathies, sought to rally the people. In June 1936 a newly formed Chinese Writers' Association, with a membership of over a hundred, adopted the slogan "Literature for National Defense";[2] and in October of the same year, writers such as Pa Chin, Lin Yutang, Mao Tun, Kuo Mo-jo, and Lu Hsün jointly issued a Literary Workers' Manifesto on the United Resistance and Freedom of Speech. After the Marco Polo Bridge Incident on July 7, 1937, these writers became even more intent on addressing themselves to the question of Japanese aggression against China. On March 27, 1938, they established the Chinese Writers' Anti-Aggression Association, and declared:

From half a year's experience of resisting the army, we have learned some invaluable lessons. For a weak country to repel aggression by a stronger country and its superior army, the people's morale must be stimulated in order to tap their vast potential. Literary writers are the craftsmen of men's souls, and literary activities are the most effective means of arousing the people.... Like the front-line soldier with his gun, we must use our pens to motivate the people. The task of defending our country is also the task of the arts.[3]

Many writers were recruited into doing propaganda work in the unoccupied interior. They wrote and staged plays, drew patriotic cartoons, wrote wall posters, sang war songs, and read poems. The Chinese Communists were particularly effective in organizing dramatic and singing troupes. War poetry proliferated, and war fiction emphasized the heroic sacrifices of Chinese soldiers, guerrilla warfare, Japanese atrocities, the tragic stories of refugees, and even war romances. Among the foremost writers were Lao She (1899–1966), Ai Wu (1904–   ), Wu Tsu-hsiang (1908–   ), Mao Tun, and Pa Chin. Lao She, as head of the Chinese Writers' Anti-Aggression Association, gave "a conspicuous example of unstinted patriotic service."[4] Ai Wu wrote about the war and the peasants in volumes of short stories, novels, and autobiographies. Wu Tsu-hsiang wrote a patriotic novel called *Ya-tsui lo* (*Duck Bill Fall*), and Mao Tun wrote *Ti-yi chieh-tuan ti ku-shih* (*Story of the First Phase*), which traced the war from its beginning to the time of the government's retreat from Shanghai.[5] As for Pa Chin, even before this period had begun, he had already written a number of short stories and essays, as well as a novel, denouncing the Japanese. For example, his 1932 novel *Dream on the Sea* attacked Japanese aggression. Now with hostilities between China and Japan in full swing, he wrote *Huan-hun ts'ao* (*The Grass of Resurrection*), which consists of three short stories, and the *Huo* (*Fire*) trilogy.

II   The Grass of Resurrection

The first of the three stories is called "Meng-na li-so" ("Mona Lisa"). The narrator tells of meeting a Frenchwoman and her child at a restaurant in Shanghai. Interpreting for the Frenchwoman and a Chinese waiter, the narrator learns that the woman, who looks like Mona Lisa, is married to a Chinese fighter pilot. The highpoint of the story is when the Frenchwoman tells the narrator, with deep emotion:

Don't think I only know personal happiness. We French are like you, the Chinese people. We, too, revere freedom, love, justice. We have never bowed to superior force.... In truth, I could say I am also a Chinese and can do whatever a Chinese woman can do. I am willing to have my husband sacrifice his life for his fellow countrymen.... If he dies in such a cause, he would be happy, and I'd bring up his son. The child is very much like his father and will do whatever his father did. I believe that the War of Resistance will continue until the people of this land are free.[6]

The second story is "Huan-hun ts'ao" ("The Grass of Resurrection"). In it, the narrator writes to a friend about his friendship with two young girls, Lisa and Chin Chia-feng, in Chungking. Chin and her mother have been killed in a bombing raid, and Lisa, distraught over the tragedy, would like to believe in the existence of the legendary "grass of resurrection" to bring her dead friends back to life. The last story, "Mou fu-fu" ("A Certain Couple"), describes the tragedy that has struck the narrator's friend Wen who has died in a bombing raid and left a wife and a young son.

These stories are by no means masterpieces of war fiction. In each the narrator is a thinly disguised Pa Chin himself; and the stories do little but voice Pa Chin's personal feelings during the early stages of the war. Their only unity comes from the war theme. "Mona Lisa" stresses the heroic sentiments of the people in resisting the invaders; "The Grass of Resurrection" is symbolic of the will and determination of the Chinese resisters; and the last, "A Certain Couple," describes a typical example of the havoc that the war has brought to an average family which otherwise would be happily together, making plans for its future.

III Fire

A more important piece of anti-Japanese fiction is Pa Chin's *Huo* (*Fire*) trilogy. Regarding the writing of it, Pa Chin said: "In writing this novel I wanted not only to communicate my fervor and express my indignation, but also to stimulate other people's courage and strengthen their faith. I also wanted them to see in the activities of these simple youths the hope for a new China."[7]

Volume I of the trilogy centers on the activities of a group of men and women living in Shanghai in 1937. All of them are "doers." They are "Pa Chin people," who live in the present with a firm belief in their cause. They are essentially nonreflective, nonseden-

tary, and willing to act. Their emotional responses are limited to
what is good for the country, and they are eager to destroy the
enemy. For instance, Feng Wen-shu and Chu Su-chen are a new
breed of women, no longer dependent on or submissive to their
elders nor to the opposite sex of any age — they are men's equals.
Serving as volunteer nurses' aides in a Shanghai military hospital,
they comfort the wounded, sing songs, and do everything in their
power to make the patients comfortable. Feng leaves Shanghai to
join a group of young men and women who are going to work as
volunteer entertainers near the front, and Chu leaves Shanghai to
work in a military hospital, also near the front. Matching the two
young women in enthusiasm is a young man named Liu Po. He
insists that the war effort is more important than anything personal. Though in love with Chu Su-chen, he has little time for
romance. With Liu are other young students, actors, artists, and
writers, all determined to do everything possible to halt or at least
slow the Japanese advance. After the Japanese occupy the Chinese
sectors of Shanghai, these young Chinese move their operations to
the city's French Concession and engage in guerrilla activities
against the Japanese. One of them, a Korean activist, assassinates a
Japanese commander, in an operation in which one of his comrades
is also killed.

Written in two months in 1941, Volume II describes the activities
of a twelve-person propaganda unit serving near the front in 1938
— presumably in the mountainous war zone of central China,
probably in Anhwei province. The unit lives in a blockhouse and
the members are in their teens and early twenties; their job is to
arouse the support of the peasants for the war effort. They write
and produce propaganda plays, sing songs with the peasants, and
conduct discussion sessions about the consequences of the Japanese
occupation. When they are not working among the peasants, they
tell each other about their past, evaluate their work, analyze their
shortcomings, and console one another regarding their homesickness. By emphasizing their youth and immaturity, Pa Chin seeks to
identify his heroes and heroines with his young readers.

Feng Wen-shu, the heroine in Volume I, and her friend Chou
Hsin are enthusiastic about their work, despite occasional spells of
homesickness. As the Japanese troops draw near, the leader of the
young comrades, Tseng Ming-yüan, in deference to majority will,
decides to take the group out of the immediate combat zone. Three
of the group decide, however, to remain in the area as guerrillas.

One of the three, a woman, explains: "...my family is finished, including my unhappy marriage. My husband is dead. Alone by myself, where would I go? What would I do? What worries would I have? ... Whether I am alive or dead makes no difference to me...."[8]

Joining refugees and soldiers, the main group retreats to the interior through the hazardous Ta-pieh Mountains in Anhwei province in the face of constant Japanese bombing attacks. During one of those attacks, one member of the group loses his hearing and another, Wang Tung, is hit by a bomb. The others always thought of Wang as a spoiled rich child, but he declares before his death that he is not sorry that he joined the group and urges the others to continue the struggle. Moved, the other members promise that they will erect a monument in his honor after the war. Finally, the group reaches Wuhan, and after contacting the military authorities, they plan to take a short trip to Hankow to buy supplies and to recruit more workers. Despite all that has happened, they are more resolved than ever to continue their work.

Volume III shifts to Canton, with the war very much in the background. Feng Wen-shu stays with Chu Su-chen, now a college student. Feng Wen-shu is haunted by images of wartime destruction and debates with T'ien Hui-shih, an elderly Chinese Christian patriot, about the existence of God and the validity of Christianity. Chu Su-chen, however, worries about Liu Po, who has remained in Shanghai. From newspaper accounts Chu Su-chen learns of the guerrilla activities against the Japanese conducted by Liu Po and the others; the reports make her worry about the safety of Liu, whom she has not seen for three years. Though she approves of the goals of the guerrillas, she wants Liu to join her in Canton and has repeatedly urged him to leave Shanghai.

Finally, Liu is allowed to leave Shanghai but is killed before his departure. Upon receiving this tragic news, Chu goes to Shanghai to avenge his death. She fails in an assassination attempt and vanishes afterwards. (In the revised edition of Volume III, the ending is changed. Chu rushes to Shanghai and learns that Liu is not dead but in jail, from which he is released. She takes him to Hong Kong, marries him, and he regains his health. A happy ending to a wartime romance.)[9]

Volume III has its allotment of undesirable characters. Continuing to show his contempt for "hollow" intellectuals, Pa Chin creates a professor named Chang Yi-mou, who admires Mussolini and other fascists; a student, Wen-chien, who engages in smuggling; a woman, Hsieh Chih-chun, who marries only for security; and another student who is very promiscuous.

Opposed to these negative characters is the middle-aged Chinese Christian patriot, T'ien Hui-shih. T'ien never wavers in his determination to see his magazine *The Pole Star* published, despite persistent money problems and difficulties with printers. At fifty-two, he is much older than Feng Wen-shu and Chu Su-chen, but fully retains his youthful spirits. Comparing himself to them, he says he does not have their spontaneous outbursts of joy or sorrow but instead has a sense of equilibrium in mind and heart. At home, he has a perfect relationship with the wife his parents chose for him. They have lived together for thirty years without ever quarreling; his relationship with his two sons is warm and affectionate. Their home life is described as follows: "When the family ate dinner, drank tea, and talked together, the whole room was permeated with peace and sweetness. Looking at one another's happy faces, the four of them shared the same feeling: 'I'm the happiest person on earth and have no demands to make of society.' All felt that there could not be any more harmonious atmosphere...."[10]

T'ien's function in Volume III is twofold. First, to present and reflect a different attitude toward the war. Even though he believes the war to be justified, his attitude toward it is markedly different from that of Liu Po or of Tseng Ming-yüan in Volumes I and II. Unlike those who uncritically support the war because of national survival, he rationalizes his support on the Christian ground that war is bad and kills, and that the publication of his magazine *The Pole Star* is an attempt to scatter the seeds of life. In short, he opposes the aggressor only because the aggressor destroys life and he loves life.

Second, by emphasizing that T'ien's family background is similar to Chüeh-hsin's in *Family,* though T'ien lacks the latter's resentfulness and bitterness toward his authoritarian father, Pa Chin seems to admit that happiness is possible in parent-arranged marriages and to have rendered his earlier harsh criticism of the family system less valid. Drawn from an actual prototype, Han-lu,[11] T'ien could very well represent a more mature Pa Chin.

The *Fire* trilogy is an expression of Pa Chin's feelings during the war. Its locales include Shanghai, the war zone, and Canton; its cast includes the admirable and the despicable. Despite the lack of moving battle scenes, exciting pictures of individual or group heroism, passionate love-making, and an exploration of the Chinese wartime psyche, the trilogy is memorable for Pa Chin's concentration on the emotions of patriotic men and women whose idealism and fiery zeal is symbolized by the title *Fire* itself.

Volume III of *Fire* was completed in 1943. Up to that time, Pa Chin's faith in his people and his country had remained steadfast. To him, people of all religious faiths could be patriotic. Mr. T'ien points out: "Christians and non-Christians are all alike. If only you believe in love and believe in truth, if only you are willing to sow the seeds of life and encourage others to seek alike, then what is the difference between you and me?"[12] This was essentially Pa Chin's position prior to his rapid transformation from an optimist into a pessimist.[13]

IV   Little People, Little Things

The Grass of Resurrection and the *Fire* trilogy sing of the patriotic deeds of men and women in glowing terms. *Hsiao-jen, hsiao-shih* (*Little People, Little Things*), a volume of five short stories, is somewhat different in its portrayal of the lives of average people trying to survive as best as they can during the last years of the war. Gone is the high-flown propaganda justifying the war. If anything, the long war has made them into Wastelanders characterized by their enervating and neurotic pettiness as well as by physical and spiritual sterility. Gone also is much of human dignity. These small people have no ideals and merely want to survive.

The setting of "Chu yü chi" ("Piglet and Chickens") is an old compound in Chungking which has been subdivided into several rental units, and its cast includes the narrator, a teenage boy, and several women. In a period of rampant inflation, Widow Feng has seen her rent raised from five *yüan* a month to nearly fifty, and a single egg now sells for a *yüan*. To fight inflation in a limited way, she tries to raise a few chickens in the communal living quarters, but this is not appreciated by her neighbors and especially not by a teenage boy who takes a perverse delight in mistreating her chickens. Often, the widow and the boy engage in a heated exchange of obscenities, followed by the mysterious death of some of her chickens. Desperate, she tries to raise a piglet, which arouses even greater opposition, not only from the boy but also from her fashionably dressed landlady, who threatens to raise her rent or evict her. Before long, her piglet also dies. As the story ends, the widow leaves the compound with the only chicken she has left.

The scene of "Hsiung yü ti" ("Brothers") is wartime Chung-king. A few flimsy huts, surrounded by a mound of refuse and debris, the skeletons of ruined houses, and a few makeshift shacks built for temporary construction workers adorn the landscape and provide the background for an inquisitive narrator to witness first a quarrel and then a fistfight between two brothers. After the fight, the elder brother murmurs to himself: "Lao-wu [Fifth Brother] is too much; he doesn't respect me. As for this latest argument, all he had to do was to tell me his problem. I could have paid him his fifty or sixty dollars. Even though we had different mothers, we are still brothers. When we quarrel and fight, we both lose face. If only he had been more understanding, shown me more respect, we would not have quarreled.... Well, I too drank a little too much...."[14] A week or so later, a house collapses, crushing five people to death. Rushing to the scene of the accident, the elder brother learns that one of the victims is his younger brother. Frantically he tries to move the beams, but his efforts are unavailing. Deeply traumatized by the loss of his brother, he returns to his house, incoherent in speech. As the curious narrator watches, the elder brother switches off the electric light, leaving a background of eerie darkness.

The story of "Fu yü ch'i" ("Husband and Wife") is structured around a street quarrel between an unhappily married couple. The man, a tailor, publicly denounces his wife before a group of spectators: "She is deliberately against me. When I say one thing, she says another. For example, when a customer wanted his work finished in five days, and I worked hard to meet the deadline, she sat on her ass. I told her to make the buttons, but she insisted on doing something else to make me miss the deadline."[15] The wife has her own bellyful of grievances: "What he said is not true at all. It is not that I like to squabble; I seldom quarrel with him, not more than once or twice a year. He went to Chi-yang in January and didn't write to me for two months, and didn't send me any money for six months. For nine months I worked for him and took care of his shop. He says I didn't do any work. If I hadn't, what would I have lived on? His shop would have been closed long ago. He didn't come home, didn't write a single letter. I even tried to lie to Mrs. Chang who lives upstairs, saying how busy he was, how he didn't have time. And when he did come home, he didn't say one kind word to me...."[16] The quarrel goes on and on.

"Nü-hai yü mao" ("A Girl and Her Cat") concerns a Cantonese

girl's devotion to her cat in wartime Kweilin. The cat is by no means extraordinary but the girl's devotion to it is . She feeds it with all types of nourishing food, but it keeps disappearing and then returning after a while. Each time it returns, she treats it more kindly; but finally it returns, in a sorry condition, for the last time. It has developed a limp, and lost much of the hair on and around its tail. In sorrow, the girl rushes out to buy pork liver and fish to feed it. But it dies and is properly buried.

"Sheng yü ssu" ("Life and Death") is about a middle-aged man who tells everyone he can about the death of his wife. Every day in his shop, wearing a neat Sun Yat-sen suit and standing by his wife's coffin, with the drums and cymbals beating, he repeats his story over and over again with the air of an incantation:

Gentlemen, I would like to report to you. My woman's illness was first diagnosed by a Dr. Huang. He is a famous gynecologist; he said my wife was four months pregnant and gave her some drugs to "stabilize her embryo." He came to see my wife at one o'clock in the morning. Later I took my wife to see another doctor at a certain hospital. Dr. Wang is very famous. He said it was not pregnancy and suggested that she have an X-ray examination, but that was on Thursday, and the hospital only had X-ray services on Mondays, Wednesdays, and Fridays. My woman didn't have a chance. But even when she was nearing death, she remained lucid. We were sleeping in the same bed. She sat up at four in the morning and told me to leave her alone. She put on her clothes and shoes but fainted when she stood up.... May I advise everyone of you. If your spouse is sick, be sure to find a good doctor. The Dr. Huang that swore my wife was pregnant ... his full name is so-and-so and he lives at such-and-such address.[17]

In all the stories, the narrator is unobtrusive and faithfully reports what he has seen and heard. His descriptions are graphic and he records accurately the language used by these small people frustrated by their problems. In addition to providing unity to the stories, he also reveals his personal development. For example, in "Piglet and Chickens" he describes himself as one who loves quietness and finds the exchange of obscenities between the widow and the boy distasteful and annoying. But sad as the widow's situation may be, he did nothing to prevent what happened, nor does he seem to be able to grasp its complete meaning. After the widow has moved out and the new tenants, relatives of the landlady, have moved in, he says: "...the landlady increased her visits to the compound. And, needless to say, the stone steps in the courtyard were very clean, forever ridden of the footprints of the piglet and the chickens."[18] His lack of concern for the involvement in that story is followed by signs of personal growth in "Brothers." After he has seen the electric light switched off in the elder brother's room, he wonders about him: "Maybe his brother's corpse has been removed, maybe it still lies by the slope under the moonlight. But what kind of dreams is the elder brother having now? Is he dreaming of squabbling with his younger brother over the blanket, threatening to break his brother's leg or hollering by his brother's body?"[19] While the same narrator may be disgusted by the quarrel between the tailor and his wife in "Husband and Wife," he is definitely sympathetic to the girl and her devotion to the cat. Passing by the cat's grave, he seems to sense the girl's loneliness.[20] More importantly, while the others listen to the widower's story with amusement in "Life and Death," he seems to be the only person who understands the true depth of the widower's bereavement.

Structurally, the five stories do not have plots in the usual sense. Instead, Pa Chin creates moods and crystallizes certain fundamental emotions in a way that few Chinese writers have ever been able to achieve. And it is these moods and these emotions that the reader remembers. The result is a series of *moments,* each complete in itself. For example, the best *moment* in "Piglet and Chickens" is when the widow leaves the compound with a lone chicken on her lap. Without editorial comment, the reader knows that the widow has been defeated by the boy and her unsympathetic neighbors. In "Brothers" the true *moment* of insight about the relationship between the two brothers occurs when the elder brother switches off his light after learning of the death of his younger brother. The street quarrel between the tailor and his wife is the *moment* of true division between the couple; the girl's utter loneliness is best represented by the cat's grave; and the widower's repeated babblings about his wife's death betray his deep sense of outrage and loss. In each *moment*, Pa Chin presents true glimpses of the anguish of the human heart. Each story reveals the essence of the central character's life as Pa Chin sees it. Also, while in each story this intimate revelation comes suddenly, sometimes in a sentence or in a paragraph; in each Pa Chin has revealed, with compassion, the deepest secret of his character's being.

V   Ward Number Four

The general mood of sickness which prevails in *Little People,*

Little Things is magnified many times in *Ti ssu ping-shih* (*Ward Number Four*). In its introduction, Pa Chin includes parts of a letter:

When I received your letter (it took four months for it to get here), a friend of mine had just died of cholera. Yet the Chief of the Health Bureau said that there was no cholera epidemic. Today, after several hundred victims have died and after the Chief has "discovered" cholera, I still see many perspiring coolies swarming around the food stalls and eating sliced watermelons, hawkers selling ice-cakes by bus stops, patrons at cafés putting ice into their glasses.... No wonder a foreign diplomat has just been infected. Living in this city is like living on the edge of a precipice that has no railing. Please thank our Health Bureau Chief for me. Because of his act, he has indirectly sent many citizens to the Kingdom of Heaven and history will gratefully record his name.[21]

This introduction establishes the tone of *Ward Number Four,* a novelette based on Pa Chin's own experience in a substandard hospital in Kweiyang in 1944.

Instead of describing the dreary existence of a number of ordinary people who try to cope with problems in different settings, *Ward Number Four* limits itself to a surgical ward of twelve beds in the interior of China. A gallstone patient records in his diary what he sees in the ward during a stay of eighteen days. What he records is a series of pictures of the ward, the staff, and the patients.

The ward is a crowded place full of beds, patients, spittoons, teapots, teacups, wooden stools, a rusty bedpan, an uneven dirt floor, paper windows, and the odor of human excrement. The doctors are impatient and indifferent to the suffering of the patients, and the nurses value themselves so highly that they seldom allow their hands to get dirty. The ward is so poorly equipped and supplied that patients have to purchase from the outside such necessary items as bandages, sugar, and even toilet paper, mostly through a janitor named Ch'eng. In fact, the ward resembles an animal kennel and is managed and controlled by the janitor, who causes and aggravates the patients' feelings of hopelessness, inadequacy, and alienation. And the patients, all of them poor, are presented in primitive terms: they scream for bedpans, holler because of their pain, and share dark and secret jokes with one another.

An indigent laborer occupies Bed Number Eleven. Though he was injured at work, his factory refuses to pay his medical bills. Since he has no money to spend in the ward, his needs are forever neglected by the janitor. When he wants the bedpan, the janitor is not around or pretends not to have heard his call, and the nurses consider it beneath their dignity to perform such a menial task. Groaning and moaning, he seems to be more like a wounded animal than a human. The narrator notes: "He could no longer clearly pronounce a single word, and no one could detect any humanlike sounds in the noises he made. His cries resembled the howling of animals. He cried and screamed, whether anyone offered him sympathy or not, whether anyone took care of him or not."[22] To prevent him from falling off the bed, he is tied to it with a rope. His misery ends one evening when he dies. His corpse is quickly removed from the ward, a piece of paper attached to his chest stating the approximate time he died. His death stirs no interest in the ward other than a frivolous remark from the patient in Bed Number Eight.

In Bed Number Two is an elderly man with a giant-sized neck tumor. A vegetarian, he is suffering from the ravages of syphilis. His life in the ward is characterized by visits from his son, who complains of the high cost of buying him nourishing food and is reluctant to be close to his father's smelly body. Like the patient in Bed Number Eleven, he only knows the reality of going to the toilet and his phobia against injections. His death also creates no ripples. Matter-of-factly, the narrator records: "There was no more trace of the man's existence in the ward. Death seems to be so common, so unfrightening, and so easy."[23]

Horror seems to be endless in the ward. The patient in Bed Number Twelve is a young man whose left eye has had to be removed because of genetic syphilis, inherited from his father. He is terribly frightened of the operation and suffers immensely after it. He moans to his plain-looking wife: "Oh, I can't see anything. I told so-and-so not to allow you come here.... Screw his old lady, I'm so pitiful...."[24] Terrified by his bleeding left eye, she wonders if he will ever be able to go back to his chauffeur's job.

Bed Number Six is occupied by a healthy-looking country lad who has come to the city to work. Originally hospitalized for a broken arm, he is now suffering from typhus, which he contracted at another hospital. As his health deteriorates, his behavior becomes more strange. He sings ditties, cries easily, and for no reason loosens the bandage on his left arm and throws off his bedcovers to exhibit his lower body. When the covers are rolled up, he immediately throws them off again. Like a naughty boy, he holds his penis in his hand and urinates in all directions. He soon dies in a delirium.

The success of the novelette lies neither in its character analysis nor in its plot development. Both receive minimal attention from Pa Chin. He spends little time inside his characters' heads. He describes for the most part, what an outsider would have seen and heard — gestures, actions, talk, and the locale itself. The result is a tribute to his keen and sensitive powers of observation — not only of noises and odors but even, more importantly, of such human actions as eating, vomiting, screaming, excreting, dying.

Nor does the presentation lack point and significance. The novelette, developed with the precision of superb photography, is a picture of decay and death. The major theme is the vitiation and degradation of the poor in a society which has put money above all other considerations. The narrator notes that the first-class patients in the same hospital receive the best of care and treatment, with servants waiting on them around the clock. Pa Chin's point seems to be that the lack of money inevitably means inhumane treatment by one's fellow human beings. What is left unspoken by Pa Chin is that this need not be, but left no doubt that it is actually so.

In short, the works discussed in this chapter represent three different phases of Pa Chin's shifting views during the war years. During the first phase, he, like many other writers, was interested in firing up the enthusiasm of the people to resist the Japanese aggressors; during the second phase, his patriotic calls for action gave way to realistic portrayals of ordinary people, as in *Little People, Little Things*. And during the third phase, as the war dragged on, his pessimism about his country grew, a pessimism reflected in *Ward Number Four*. Like Chekhov's *Ward Number Six, Ward Number Four* was intended to be a microcosmic picture of the larger sickness in the whole society.[25] Because of its negative portrayal of people and conditions existing in the interior of China, it was banned by the Nationalist government.

CHAPTER 6

Leisure Garden

I N 1941, Pa Chin returned to Chengtu, his childhood home, for a visit of fifty days, during which time he learned that many of his old friends had either died or moved away. At a dinner party, he heard of the recent death of his notorious fifth uncle, who had squandered away the family fortune on gambling, women, and other vices and had been thrown out of his home by his wife and son. No one seemed to care much about his uncle; never close to him, Pa Chin at first was also rather indifferent to the news of his death. But nostalgic as he was, he remembered the details of his uncle's life and began to toy with the idea of building a novel around it as a sequel to *Autumn,* a continuation of the story of the decline of a traditional family. The idea became a reality in 1944, when he wrote a novel called *Ch'i-yüan* (*Leisure Garden*), whose title was taken from one of the pavilions in his grandfather's compound.

I *Structure and Theme*

Structurally, the novel has two centers of interest: the life and death of Yang Lao-shan, who resembles Pa Chin's fifth uncle, and the rise of a new family, represented by a fictional character named Yao Kuo-tung, and his family. Yang Lao-shan's miserable past is revealed in bits and pieces by his former servants and told in "flashback" form by Yang's younger son; Yang's present life, leading to his death, runs simultaneously with the story of Yao Kuo-tung's family, culminating in the death of Yao's son. These two centers are separate and are connected primarily by the narrator, who occupies a central position in the novel, being in touch with all the other characters and therefore capable of tying the strands of the story together. As the novel opens, he moves into his old friend

Yao's Leisure Garden estate as a guest of Yao and his wife. A sensitive and inquisitive man, he soon becomes interested in the story of the previous owner of the estate, Yang Lao-shan. Thus he becomes at once witness, narrator, and actor. A second device that links the two plots together is character analogies. For instance, Yang Lao-shan and Yao Kuo-tung's son have many things in common. Both are children of rich and indulgent parents, and both die near the end of the novel; and both deaths could have been avoided had they had responsible parents with a proper sense of discipline. Two other characters with similarities are Yang Lao-shan's long-suffering and obedient wife and Yao Kuo-tung's young wife. Though these two women are a generation apart in age, they are in reality twins in bondage, bound by the traditional demands made of Chinese women.

The novel has three major themes: the evils of wealth, the status of women, and the father-and-son relationship. In *Little People, Little Things* and *Ward Number Four,* one of the major causes for suffering is the lack of money; the misuse of money is viewed as the root of evil in *Leisure Garden.* During Pa Chin's visit to Chengtu, what struck him was the continued existence of the wealthy, who still lived recklessly without much regard for others.[1] As a reaction to his hatred of the rich leisure class, he intends to show that the rich are damned and implies that the common man's dream of having wealth is, in reality, a thinly veiled nightmare. In other words, the novel is a critique of Chinese society in the 1940s; and he pronounces a sentence of doom over a social order that imagines itself in full flower, a theme he develops through the setting, the characterizations, and the final tragedies of Yang Lao-shan and Yao's son.

Central to the novel's total effect are symbols of enclosure, self-complacency, and insensitivity. These symbols are represented by the setting, by Mrs. Chao, and by Yao Kuo-tung, respectively. From the outset, the setting is charged with symbolic overtones. Chapter three begins with a description of Leisure Garden: "A high wall made of gray bricks, a glossy lacquered front door. Two big characters, 'Ch'i Yüan,' written in classic calligraphic style and each the size of a wash basin, stared down from the door's lintel."[2] Leisure Garden is one of the last bastions of tradition; its formidable door shields its inhabitants from the outside world and seeks to guard their secrets. As long as its residents stay within, they shall never get to know either themselves or others.

The next symbol is the rich Mrs. Chao, who is the mother of Yao's deceased first wife. She never actually appears in the novel but is reported as having done this or that and, therefore, seems more like a phantom than a real person. Nevertheless, her presence is deeply felt by everyone. She exercises complete control over Yao's son, nicknamed Tiger, whom she teaches the joys of gambling and how to snub servants and poor relatives. She disdains Yao's second wife and makes the young woman's life miserable, and she commands the respect of Yao and the awe of all the servants. Her hold over everyone lies in her wealth, which has made her into an omnipresent deity — selfish, faceless, and mean.

If Mrs. Chao personifies the evils of money, Yao Kuo-tung is the personification of insensitivity. He has studied abroad, served as an official of government, been a college professor, has translated a book, and he is now the owner of the luxurious Leisure Garden; but his real desire is simply to perpetuate his pleasant life. The narrator sees these different facets to Yao's character and notes such apparent contradictions as Yao's mourning the sad state of society while being uncritical of his own role in it, and his frequent references to high ideals and strict principles while living lavishly on the family inheritance and being extremely obsequious toward his rich mother-in-law. It seems to Pa Chin that the luxury of Leisure Garden definitely deters Yao from seeing any possibilities in life except ones which are conceived in material terms. For example, he has a beautiful and sensible second wife, whom he regards solely as a decorative item; when he sees the son of the previous owner plucking flowers in Leisure Garden, he doesn't even have enough curiosity to find out why. Though he is aware of the tragedy that has befallen the previous owner, he draws no lesson from it in the training of his own son. He makes excuses for his son's unruly behavior, and indulges his every whim. His insensitivity to all things other than his material goods and his status in society is indirectly responsible for his son's accident and death. He and his mother-in-law represent the "ins" of the degenerate Chengtu society of the 1940s, but their senses have been so dulled that they understand neither their own world of inherited wealth nor any world outside it.

The victims of this sickness and corruption are the children. Yang Lao-shan had been so spoiled by his rich parents that his life could only end in death and disgrace. Tiger, the undisciplined son of Yao Kuo-tung, dies in a drowning accident. Though it is an accident that might have been avoided, Pa Chin's thesis seems to be that this is not very important since if the Yaos had continued their way of life, Tiger would, in any event, have grown up and died as another Yang Lao-shan. To the narrator, the novel ends with his recognition of the forces that made Yang Lao-shan and Tiger what they were. Presumably, Pa Chin hoped that the novel might show others who live and think like the Yaos what the consequences of their thoughtless use of wealth could be.

A second theme of the novel is the oppressed status of women. The two women Pa Chin uses as symbols are a generation apart in age, but both live under oppressive male domination. The old Mrs. Yang is a typical example of her age who questions neither the condition nor the role of women and who tolerates her husband's repeated misconduct. Even after she finds that he has lied to her again and again, she almost instinctively forgives him and hopes for the best. Later, she is forced to agree to her elder son's demand that her husband move out of the house permanently, because she depends upon her elder son for a living. Her superhuman tolerance of her husband and her obedience of her elder son are characteristic of a traditional Chinese woman whose role has been prescribed by tradition. Never taught that she has a right to satisfy her own needs, she could see no other alternative than to tolerate her husband; and without any means of supporting herself, she has no choice but to agree to her son's harsh demand.

She may appear as a stereotype or a caricature in most of the novel, but she becomes surprisingly real as a person in the following episode. One night when her husband comes home late as usual, she drags her sons out of bed and instructs them to kneel before him, begging him to save some money for them to live on. When he looks embarrassed, she presses on: "Why are you so speechless today? Are you embarrassed? They're your children. You are a father and should behave like one. They need you to be an example to them. Tell them that the money you're squandering was earned by you, and was not the money you inherited...."[3] Blushing with embarrassment, he asks her to forgive and to forget. She becomes even more agitated: "You love to quarrel with me. Why're you afraid of quarreling today? If you can do all those things, can't I at least talk about them? Who doesn't know that you whore around and gamble? Everyone knows what I have to put up with." Covering his ears, he begs her not to say any more and offers to kowtow to her. She stops him and says: "Let me kowtow to you, let me kowtow to you. But take pity on us three, mother and children. It would be better to kill us than to let us suffer like this.''[4]

Mrs. Yao Kuo-tung, Yao's second wife, fares no better than Mrs. Yang. Though she lives in a luxurious house and is waited on by servants, she is a caged bird. Her husband is not irresponsible like Yang Lao-shan, but he neither understands her nor cares to. Sharing little in common with him, she feels compelled to describe her background to a stranger — the narrator. Consisting of nothing more than an old-fashioned mother and brother and limited contacts with schoolmates and the world at large, it defines her existence. Her attempt to broaden her horizon through her marriage to Yao proves to be illusory. After marriage to him, she spends most of her time either reading fiction or going to the movies. Living with an insensitive husband, the possibility that she will ever realize her potential is small indeed. Her inability to help herself is compounded by her inability to help her stepson; she can merely watch him go from bad to worse. Her lack of influence with her husband is similar to Mrs. Yang's helplessness in preventing Yang Lao-shan from becoming a complete wastrel.

Pa Chin's attitude toward both women is sympathetic. Commenting on the young Mrs. Yao, he wrote: ''I truly felt sympathetic toward good-natured women like her. I thought to myself that if they could have lived in a different society and under a different system, their youth might have produced beautiful fruit, and their intelligence and talent would have had the chance to develop themselves fully. In any case, they would not have become parasites of society as they did in the old society.''[5] This might well have also included old Mrs. Yang.

It is interesting to note that the young Mrs. Yao is presented primarily as a misunderstood housewife and as Tiger's frustrated stepmother. She is radically different from the young women in Pa Chin's earlier fiction — those who publish journals, lead demonstrations, participate in patriotic activities, advocate free love, and so forth. Could it be that by the mid-1940s Pa Chin, now a married man himself, had modified his earlier views of the role of women in society? That he saw women primarily as housewives? That now his version of a happy modern family was limited to a wife who was well provided for and understood by her spouse? Could this shift in viewpoint also signal a transition in Pa Chin's interests from political themes to more mundane ones such as family relationships?

The novel's last major theme is the father-son relationship, of which it contains three sets. First, there are Yang Lao-shan's father and Yang Lao-shan himself; second, Yao Kuo-tung and his son Tiger; and third, Yang Lao-shan and his two sons. Yang Lao-shan's father does not actually appear in the novel but his influence is reflected in what Yang Lao-shan is. The fact that Yang is a wastrel is attributable to his father's neglect and laxness in disciplining him. Yang Lao-shan's death has its roots in his early family training, or in other words, Yang Lao-shan's end is doomed from the beginning. Similarly, Yao Kuo-tung's turning over to his mother-in-law, Mrs. Chao, his parental responsibility for the guidance of Tiger is a clear abrogation of his duty as a father. Yang Lao-shan's father and Yao are, by implication, unintentional murderers of their own offspring, even though they themselves don't realize the extent of their failures as fathers. Continuing to the next generation the lack of parental discipline Yang Lao-shan also fails his own children.

The consequences of parental irresponsibility evoke different responses from the sons. These include Yang Lao-shan's feelings of guilt and repentance, Tiger's complete ignorance of the evil that his father has done to him, and mixed feelings of hatred and love among Yang Lao-shan's children. Pa Chin does not fully develop the responses of Yang Lao-shan and Tiger to their respective fathers, but he dwells on the love-hate reaction of Yang's two children to their father.

Yang Lao-shan's elder son is unique among Pa Chin's range of characters. In his unkindness to his own father, he exceeds Chüeh-hui or any other rebellious character in the *Turbulent Stream* trilogy. By traditional Chinese standards, he would be considered most unfilial and could even have been sentenced to death during the Ch'ing dynasty (1644–1911). The following two excerpts show the depth of his hatred toward his father.

One night his father comes home late as usual and gives the excuse that he has been with friends. Replying to the lame excuse, the son lashes out vehemently: "Always lying. What is this nonsense about seeing friends? Who doesn't know that you went to see that [whore] Lao-wu? When we first asked you to live with us, you gave us so many excuses.... You've always lied, all for that whore. I really thought that you'd never want to come home, never want to see us. Who knows that heaven has eyes. Your precious darling deserted you and ran away with someone else. After she had stolen all your valuables and left you, you came home to us. It's a home you didn't want, among people whom you've always disliked.... I demand to know what your intentions are. Are you trying to defraud mother of some more of her money to take another concubine and rent a separate apartment? I advise you not to have such vain hopes. I'll not allow you to mistreat her anymore."[6]

And later when his father speaks of repentance, the son ridicules him: "Repentance? If you had any, you'd not have come home in the first place. Get out of this house. I don't want to have a father like you. I don't recognize you as my father."[7] The elder son, to use Freudian terms, expresses a definite need to reject parental, specifically paternal, authority. The rage he expresses is not only verbal but is also acted upon — in his expulsion of his father from the house.

But balancing the elder son's rejection is the younger son's unqualified love for the father. The younger son never speaks ill of his irresponsible father, and in the following excerpt fully reveals his love and understanding:

When I was little, my father loved me the most. I remember how he took me to bed with him ever since I was three years old. My mother liked my brother, and my brother never obeyed father. My father stayed out of the house during the day and only came home late at night. When he did come home, he'd quarrel with my mother, sometimes fiercely, and she'd always cry. But the next morning father'd say a few nice words to her, and she'd be happy again. But two or three days later, they'd quarrel again. I hated listening to their quarrels. My brother sometimes took my mother's side. I'd hide in the bed; even on hot summer days, I'd cover my head with a quilt, too scared to make a noise or to fall asleep. Later when father crawled into bed, he pulled back the covers and seeing that I wasn't asleep, would ask if I had been disturbed by his quarrels. I couldn't say anything, but merely nodded my head. He'd look at me and promise that he'd never quarrel with mother again. Seeing his tears, I cried too; I didn't dare to cry loudly, only softly. He'd console me with sweet words and then I'd fall asleep.[8]

It is interesting that in his presentation of the two different children, Pa Chin contrasted the themes of rejection and tolerance of paternal authority, probably thus revealing his own inner discord. The novel may be seen as an expression of Pa Chin's deepest emotional needs or, again in Freudian terms, the conflict between his own id and his superego — i.e., his own Oedipal conflict and his guilt complex. He hadn't yet found an answer to this obsessive question — the relationship of the child to the family — and it would continue to haunt him.

II *The Repentant Reprobate*

Besides the exploration of the different themes in the novel, a small part of its success lies in Pa Chin's portrayal of a repentant reprobate, a betrayer of hearth and home, in the person of Yang Lao-shan. Yang is based on Pa Chin's fifth uncle. But Pa Chin's fictional creation is a much better human being than his uncle ever was. What makes Yang different is his capacity for repentance, which begins almost imperceptibly. When his brothers try to force him to join them in selling the family compound, he refuses to go along and protests violently against the sale.[9] His protest is, of course, ineffective, but it does show his potential for good. No longer exercising the authority of a father, he can only watch his elder son sign the papers for him, an act which strips him totally of his parental authority.

His repentance also involves a deep sense of shame for his deeds. Strolling in the Leisure Garden with his younger son, he holds the boy's hand and says: "This is my retribution. I'm unworthy to be your father, unworthy of you.... Remember my words. Don't be like me. Don't be like your worthless father...."[10]

Ironically, it is the expulsion from his home by his elder son that marks the real turning point in his life. From then on, he is truly aware of how badly he has sinned, and this recognition sets in motion the possibility of his redemption; thereafter he goes from guilt to mortification to redemption. As a first step he moves to a decrepit temple, which is the symbolic vestment of his corrupt existence. Seeking to cut himself off from the past, he pretends to be a mute. But the temple is no sanctuary in which he can achieve redemption. He is never far enough away from his loving younger son; later it is the narrator who brings him love and sympathy.

Redemption requires that Yang cut his ties with his younger son and leave the sanctuary. When the son and the narrator try to get him to enter a hospital because he is ill, he goes away, leaving a note for his younger son: "Forget me. Think of me as though I were dead. You'll never find me. Let me spend the rest of my days in peace."[11] After he leaves the temple, he engages in a series of penitential mortifications. He becomes a thief and tries to live the worst possible kind of life. He eats only enough to keep himself alive and exposes himself to cold, dirt, and sickness. Soon he is arrested and assigned to a work crew. One day he sees the narrator in the street and is afraid of being followed and his location disclosed to his younger son; therefore, he refuses to work and is beaten severely by the guards. But apparently none of these self-inflicted punishments is enough to bring redemption. To be redeemed he must die.

Withdrawing from humanity, Yang contracts typhoid and dies three days later. Wrapped in a straw mat he is buried in an unknown location and his death passes virtually unnoticed. But it has a great impact on the narrator, who alone knows Yang's secret. The narrator glimpses beyond the barrier of life to the good in Yang, which implies, of course, the good in everyone. The narrator, has, through Yang Lao-shan, seen both the evil and the good in man; the process of Yang's redemption completes, for the narrator, his knowledge of that facet of human character.

III   *The Narrator*

The narrator is a crucial structural device, bridging the gap between the Yao and Yang households; he is also a device to influence the reader's judgment of what is going on, and his sensibility and intelligence mediate between the action and the reader. The narrator is also a way for Pa Chin to disengage himself from his subject and maintain an impersonal attitude toward his material without sacrificing sharpness of focus. Of equal importance, in a way, to the other themes in *Leisure Garden* is the story of the narrator, of how he develops a knowledge of life and himself.

The narrator describes himself as a professional writer who has not been in Chengtu for sixteen years. "Even though this is the place where I was brought up, it did not seem to welcome me. I didn't find one familiar face in the street. . . . Like a stranger, I lived in a small hotel, and paid a high price for a small, stinky, dim and sunless room."[12] By chance he meets his old friend Yao in the street and accepts Yao's invitation to live in Leisure Garden. Amidst its splendor, the narrator notices the strange behavior of a young boy who comes into the garden, picks one flower, and leaves. When he asks Yao about the boy, he is told that the boy's last name is Yang and that he is the son of the former owner, Yang Lao-shan.

The narrator becomes vaguely aware of the uneasy crosscurrents of past evils and present discontent that underlie the superficial prosperity of Yao's way of life. He detects an air of falseness about it all, but he is not certain of his feelings. He hears Yang Lao-shan's name mentioned by servants, and the next day he catches a glimpse of "a man's back, a long skinny body with excessively long hair, in a greasy grey-cloth padded gown."[13] When the man sees him, the man walks away quickly. With his curiosity aroused, he follows the man to the Temple of the Big Immortal, a place sharply different from the Leisure Garden. He then notices that "in a short, stout glass bottle was a single flower, the one plucked by the boy the day before,"[14] and that the sole resident of the temple is the man that he has followed. When he tries to communicate with the man, the man appears to be a mute and responds with hand gestures. Upon noticing that the man's features are similar to those of the boy he saw the day before, he concludes that the "mute" before him must be Yang Lao-shan, the boy's father.

Meanwhile, at Leisure Garden, the son of his host, Tiger, shows himself to be unruly, undisciplined, and abusive to the servants; host Yao boasts of his good relationship with the rich mother of his first wife; and the hostess, the present Mrs. Yao, a charming young woman, confesses her lack of social experience and expresses the desire to live a fuller life. In discussing one of the narrator's novels, she suggests that an author should bring some happiness into the world. This casual remark makes the narrator seriously question his role as a writer and he thinks to himself: "For the first time I recognized my own impotence and failure. My life, my writing, my plans were all a waste. I have added more sorrow to mankind; I filled many innocent eyes with tears. In this sorrow-laden world I did not bring my readers laughter. I enclosed myself in my chosen mini-world and lived selfishly, wasting my youth on sheets of white paper while forever telling the reader those sad tales. . . ."[15]

Bored with his sedentary but comfortable life at Leisure Garden and interested in helping others, the narrator decides to find out more about Yang Lao-shan, but no one can give him much information. With persistence, he coaxes the young Yang boy to tell him about his family's disgraceful past. Deeply moved by what he has heard, he becomes sympathetic toward Yang. No longer fully immersed in his work, he would like to help Yang. As a first sign of his commitment to Yang, he tries to get Yang to enter a hospital when he learns that Yang is ill. Just then, Yang disappears from the temple, apparently so as not to embarrass his younger son. However, the narrator's desire to help Yang only becomes stronger and he promises the young boy that he will try to find his father.

Time goes by and one day he sees a group of more than thirty convicts marching together, clean shaven and without shoes. One of them he recognizes as Yang Lao-shan. He calls after Yang but gets no response. He seeks Yao's assistance to find Yang. After additional investigation, the narrator learns that Yang has recently died and been buried.

Feeling totally helpless, the narrator lies to Yang's son and denies having seen his father or having any knowledge of the father's whereabouts. His act of lying is similar to Marlowe's lying to Kurtz's Intended in Joseph Conrad's *Heart of Darkness*. Like Marlowe, he probably felt that the truth would have been too dismal, too despondent for the boy to hear. In his attempt to spare the boy more grief, he ironically deprives the boy of the chance of knowing the truth about his father.

Unable to help either Yang Lao-shan or the young boy to face the truth, the narrator also cannot help his host. Having talked to Yao many times about the latter's failure as a father, the narrator is very sad to learn that Tiger has been drowned in a swimming accident. The narrator finally understands his inability to help others; and what he had intended not to do — to write more sad or sorrowful tales — is only again what he must do: to tell of the decline of both the Yang and the Yao families.

IV *Evaluation*

Leisure Garden is an interesting piece of work. Casual critics may fault its superficial handling of themes and characters,[16] but a careful reading produces a different impression. Its structure, built on two centers of interest, is directly related to its thematic content; and the use of the narrator is a clever device. By framing the whole novel in the tightly packed events of a few weeks, Pa Chin achieves the most in narrative economy. Using the narrator-observer-actor to tell the story, he achieves distance from his materials. And letting the narrator tell the story in retrospect provides a natural device for the selection of details and the organization of the plot.

Thematically, he handles the problem of money more subtly than he has elsewhere. No longer simply haranguing the reader about its evils, he shows how money has become a deterrent to an understanding by the rich of themselves and of others. In dealing with the question of women, he demonstrates how little their status has changed since the May Fourth period. The young Mrs. Yao has different goals and wants different things of life than does old Mrs. Yang, but essentially she is as bound to her husband and to her environment as Mrs. Yang ever was. And in his exploration of the father-and-son relationship, he negates his earlier belief that the family system is unmitigated evil and suggests that the family is a place where different types of human relationships can grow, and that human relationships are too diverse and too complex to be neatly categorized.

In terms of characterization, Mrs. Chao, Mrs. Yang, and Mrs. Yao are stereotypes, but they serve their functions well in the novel. Yao Kuo-tung and his son provide the necessary backdrop for the illumination of the more complex relationships within the three generations of the Yang family: Yang Lao-shan's father, Yang Lao-shan himself, and Yang's children. Just as the story of Yao Kuo-tung and his family is necessary for an intelligent understanding of the Yang family, Yang Lao-shan's family story is necessary for the narrator to achieve a true understanding of his own role in life. Thus, the complete meaning of *Leisure Garden* is based on knowledge of all its parts, each contributing its share to the total picture.

Ultimately, apart from its technical skills, what fascinates the thoughtful reader about the book is what it reveals about Pa Chin's own psyche. In his presentation of the dichotomies of rejection-acceptance and hate-love in Yang's two children, he may be expressing his own contradictory points of view toward the family, an object of scorn and scathing attack in his earlier works but now the place where love grows between an affectionate child and his irrespponsible father. Could it be that the writing of *Leisure Garden* was really an exorcism through which Pa Chin worked out the pent-up emotions that he had kept within himself all those years? Obviously he did not find a complete answer to his obsession, for he continued to explore its ramifications in his next major work, *Cold Nights*.

CHAPTER 7

Cold Nights

I F *Ward Number Four* is depressing, then *Han-yeh* (*Cold Nights*) is, no pun intended, chilling. Dealing again with the weariness induced by the long war, Pa Chin based his novel on his personal experiences in Chungking, the provisional capital of the Nationalist government, during the last year of the Sino-Japanese War.[1] For page after page, he stresses Chungking's runaway inflation, high unemployment, epidemics, starvation, indifference of the government toward her people, and the bankruptcy of people's morale and morals.

To make these facts of life real, Pa Chin carefully notes the prohibitive costs of medical care, of tuition fees, and even of the cost of a birthday cake. He emphasizes the difficulties Wang Wen-hsüan, a college-educated man, has in trying to find any job other than the one he has in a publishing company which pays him such a meager salary. And Pa Chin skillfully describes the plight of small shopkeepers and the dire distress of the refugees who poured into Chungking from all parts of the war-torn country. He contrasts this with the relative well-being of minor bureaucrats such as Chief Editor Chou and Department Chief Ch'en, and notes ironically that government propaganda all the while has been extolling the "improvement" in the people's conditions and the "progress" made in human rights.

To Pa Chin, the most frightening aspect of the war was the demoralization of a people noted for their neighborliness, kindness, and charity. They have simply become callous and cruel. He exemplifies this in the way Wang, a sick and dying man, is treated by both his superiors and his colleagues. More starkly, Wang's schoolmate, T'ang Pai-ch'ing, is so despairing of life that he commits suicide by running in front of a truck. After the war, people remark with indignation that the "victory is for them, not for us,"

128

and that living seems to have become even more difficult and their future even more uncertain.

Wang Wen-hsüan dies a few days after the victory, and his fate represents the symbolic death of all those who, like he, cherished hopes for a better China and a better tomorrow. In utter despair, Pa Chin seems to suggest that with Wang's death there also died the fires of the revolutionary radicals, the rebels against the old family system, and the anti-Japanese patriots. Furthermore, he seems to suggest that there will be no hope for China if its postwar civilization is merely a continuation of what it had been before the war. To him, the future holds no promises, only vague possibilities, glimpses of which are captured in the last paragraphs of the novel, in which an indecisive Shu-sheng faces an uncertain future:

The dead was no more, and the living gone. Even if she waited until the next day, and probably found her husband's gravesite, could she find her son? Could she change her present situation? What should she do? Search for her mother-in-law and her son? Or go back to Lanchow and accept the hand of another?

She had two weeks of vacation, and she must decide within that time: twelve or thirteen days.... But why stand in front of the stall and be battered by a chilly wind?

"I still have time to decide," she told herself and walked away slowly and steadily. And suddenly while walking in the darkness she was overcome by a curious feeling. She glanced from time to time at both sides of the street as if afraid that the quivering acetylene lights at the stalls might be extinguished by the chilly wind. The night was indeed too cold....[2]

As much as any other piece of writing by Pa Chin, *Cold Nights* stands out as one of his masterpieces, perhaps the masterpiece. It demonstrates an artistic maturity rarely seen in his previous works. Technically, it maintains the feeling of doom throughout through its use of the images of the dark and lonely night and the change of seasons; it gives the reader a feeling of participating in the action through its use of scene; it presents the conflicts among the major characters through dialogue; and it reveals the psyches of these characters through monologue. All these devices contribute to the suffocating intensity of the novel while they deepen the reader's understanding of the members of a modern Chinese family.

I *Night and the Change of Seasons*

Readers of *Cold Nights* are likely to be overwhelmed by the consistent and persistent atmosphere of doom which is skillfully achieved by Pa Chin through the use of one principal image: night. Through thirty chapters and an epilogue, daytime scenes are limited to six chapters (3, 4, 5, 9, 17, and 25); and only eight (chapters 11, 12, 13, 14, 20, 26, 27, and 29) contain both day and night scenes. The other seventeen (a majority of the chapters) are set at night.

To convey a feeling of doom, Pa Chin stresses gloominess, dimness, and darkness. Even during the daytime, the sun never shines, the sky remains gloomy, cloudy, and threatens rain. His nights are usually dark and cold, the settings dimly lit. The novel begins with a dark street scene:

...The streets were quiet and dark.... Like a piece of faded black cloth, it hovered over the earth. Apart from the dark silhouettes of a few tall structures, he could see nothing.... The chilly night air, seeping through his thinly lined gown, made him shiver slightly.... he saw the gleam of a flashlight in the distance ... but the light immediately went out. He was again enveloped in hazy darkness, the chilly air tingling his spine. He shuddered....[3]

The dark street scene is soon replaced by the entrance to Wang's apartment building. It is described as cavelike, its roundish door "was open and a roundish red doorlight glowed dimly." And Wang's two-room apartment "seemed larger and disarranged; and the electric lights particularly yellowish."[4] The apartment is subjected to frequent interruptions in the electric power, and when one occurs, Wang and his mother have to use a candle. The following is typical of the many occasions when there is no electricity:

Immediately all was dark, but after their eyes adjusted to it, some hazy gray light could be seen.... The flickering light created dark shadows and images everywhere. Blown by the wind, the candle's wax was guttering like flowing water. The makeshift candlestick — a broken teacup turned upside down — stuck on the table amidst piles of melted wax.[5]

The streets outside the apartment are also without light or at best have a "few isolated lights amidst a background of darkness because the surrounding areas were scheduled for a blackout."[6]

If all the settings are dark or nearly dark, some of the characters in the novel, many of whom are unidentified, are shadowlike. They are the shadows crouching in the dark in chapter one, a handful of pedestrians moving hastily in the cold wind, the children who lie outside Wang's apartment building in the cold, the refugees in the epilogue, or Mrs. Chang holding a candle in her hand, walking up the stairs.

And then there are the noises of the night: the sound of rats chewing on the wooden floor, T'ang Pai-ch'ing's wife shrieking for her husband, a woman's tragic voice wailing for the spirit of a sickly child to come home and the haunting voice of an old hawker selling hot water and fried rice-cakes every night.

Night is the time for troubled and fertile dreams. Wang has a series of them, beginning with one extensively described in chapter two, wherein his wife, Shu-sheng, leaves him after an argument with his mother. The nightmare itself foreshadows the novel's ending. As it progresses, Wang's body deteriorates physically, though his mind becomes ever more active. Lying in bed, he has many other nightmares. In each, his wife runs away with someone, or he or his mother dies. In one of these dreams, right after his friend T'ang's suicide, "gigantic shadows flashed before his eyes, including that of T'ang Pai-ch'ing's dark, thin face with its bloodshot eyes." Ceaselessly, he keeps hearing T'ang's final words: "I'm finished, all finished."[7] Frightened, he starts to run in his dream and is unable to stop even though he is dead tired. He runs into a dark forest, desperately searching for light. He finds some light but it comes from trees that are in flames. The fire gets hotter as it gets closer to him and finally begins to scorch his clothes. In desperation, he yells: "Help, help."[8]

It is at night or in the very early morning that Shu-sheng leaves Wang Wen-hsüan to go to Lanchow. Her departure marks the end of Wang's hopes and begins the last stage of his life. It is also at night that T'ang Pai-ch'ing's wife dies in childbirth, T'ang is killed by a truck, and Uncle Chung and Wang Wen-hsüan die in a hospital and at home, respectively.

The dark and dismal settings not only serve as decorative backdrops to enhance the atmosphere of doom, they are also an important structural device, giving unity to the book. For instance, the first paragraph of the epilogue is similar to the first paragraph of the novel: "There was a blackout throughout the mountainous city: the generators needed overhauling. After rain in the morning, it suddenly grew chilly in the afternoon, with gusts of cold wind sweeping through the city. The chilly wind had driven the customers away from the stalls. The smell of the acetylene lamps penetrated everywhere, and the flickering lights seemed also to be shuddering in this lonely, blustery night."[9] Whereas Wang, in chapter one, hears disgruntled voices from dark corners of the street, a lonely Shu-sheng in the epilogue overhears passersby commenting and complaining about how little their life has improved since the Japanese surrender. Similarly, as Wang shivers in his thinly lined gown in chapter one, Shu-sheng in the epilogue "shivered again. She felt chilled all over, as if she had been placed in an ice-cellar.... She glanced from time to time at both sides of the street as if afraid that the quivering acetylene lights at the stalls might be extinguished by the chilly wind. The night was indeed too cold."[10] The novel has come full circle. Wang and the others have died, but the people remain groping in the dark, uncertain of the future.

The dark night is also symbolic. The weak, erratic supply of electricity is symbolic of the ties that keep Wang's family together. One evening when the light goes out, Wang grumbles: "No electricity again.... They seem never to give you enough light." To which his wife replies: "Light, do you want light too?"[11] implying a connection between the yellowish light and her own life. On another occasion, looking at the lone dangling light bulb in the living room, she comments: "The·bulb seems to symbolize our life.... It has never been full of light, it never burns out completely, it simply drags on and on."[12]

The misery drags on. There is little light. One of the more prominent lights is the flashlight, used on three different occasions, strategically placed in the novel: first in chapter one, then when Shu-sheng leaves her husband in chapter twenty-three, and for the last time in the epilogue, when Shu-sheng uses it to guide her way out of the apartment building. The other lights in the novel are the weak and smelly acetylene lamps of the hawkers; the bright lights at the International Café, where luxury items such as chewing gum, chocolates, American candy, and birthday cakes are prominently displayed in the window; and the powerful lights at the Cantonese restaurant, where a party is being held in honor of Director Chou's birthday and the participants are busy currying favor with him. Night and darkness dominate the book and typify the lives of many of its characters, particularly that of Wang Wen-hsüan.

In addition to using light as a principal image in the novel, Pa Chin uses the change of the seasons to mirror the inner condition of the central characters. The novel begins in the fall and ends in the fall, covering the cycle of one year. The fall is a season which suggests the withering of a dying relationship, as suggested by Wang's frequent feelings of chill; winter is the longest season in Pa Chin's bleak world. Throughout the almost endless winter, Wang, his mother, and his wife suffer continuously. During the winter, Wang discovers the seriousness of his illness, loses his job, and his wife leaves him; his mother's resentment of her daughter-in-law increases her worries about the future of her seriously ill son; and the wife, Shu-sheng, agonizes about whether to go to Lanchow. Spring proves to be illusory. Wang's health fails to improve; Mother's hopes about her son's recovery prove to be false; and Shu-sheng's hopes of finding the happiness which has evaded her prove groundless. Summer kills Wang. It is on a late summer day that he dies; summer also brings total despair to his mother, who has lost not only her son but the sole means of her support. But it is once again in the fall that Shu-sheng returns to the city, only to find her husband dead and to become vaguely aware that she has been victimized by a romantic illusion. And another winter is coming, another season of pain and uncertainty, like the previous long winter in that two-room apartment with her husband, her mother-in-law, and her son.

II *Use of Scene*

In addition to utilizing to the full the images of night and the change of seasons to convey a sense of doom and the inner conditions of his characters, Pa Chin uses summary and scene for narration. His general method is to keep summary to the barest essential minimum, and to use scene to dramatize very intense moments, such as Shu-sheng's departure for Lanchow. The following rather lengthy extract begins with an anxious Wang waiting for his wife to come home from a party on the eve of her departure, continues with Shu-sheng's packing, and ends with their actual farewell. Its detailed description of the characters' every move and thought helps to make it one of the most memorable and pathetic scenes in the whole book.

"Shu-sheng, are you actually leaving me?" he asked again, hoping to hear in reply: "No, Hsüan, I'll never leave you." But there was no answer, the only sound to be heard being the sad cry of the old street hawker selling hot water and fried rice-cakes. His was a weak, hollow, lonely voice which barely penetrated into the room. Hsüan imagined himself a poor old man, neck drawn into his collar, his back hunched and his hands tucked into the sleeves of a torn, greasy cotton-padded gown which could not protect him from the howling wind....

Then he spent some time fantasizing and sobbing. Fortunately, his mother did not hear him, and therefore did not come to console him. Slowly he regained his composure and eventually heard footsteps in the corridor. Her footsteps. Excitedly he uncovered his tear-stained face and when his wife came in, he had turned to face the wall.

Assuming that he was asleep, Shu-sheng switched on the light and tip-toed to the rattan chair. She sat down, changed into her slippers, combed her hair with the help of a small mirror which she had taken out of a drawer, and put some things that were in the drawer in one of the suit-cases. Everything was done with a minimum of noise. Before she finished her packing, she suddenly thought of something else and went over to the bed where she watched him silently.

He was fully aware of her every move and knew that she was standing by him. He thought that she would go away very soon, but she stood there for quite a while. Unable to bear it any longer he coughed a little and, pretending that he had just awakened, turned over, yawned and opened his eyes.

"Hsüan," she said apologetically. "I'm late. How long have you been sleeping?"

He lied: "I guess I must have just fallen asleep."

"I planned to come home early, but the dinner was late. Afterwards my friends insisted on having coffee at a different place. I very much wanted to be with you, but they wouldn't let me go."

"I know," he interrupted. "Your friends must be unwilling to see you leave." This was meant as a casual remark devoid of any sarcasm.

"Are you unhappy that I came home late?" she asked gently. "I thought about you all evening, and I'd have liked so much to be with you. What I was afraid was...." She looked toward the little room in which her mother-in-law slept.

"I know. I'm not blaming you," he said. "Are you all packed?"

"Almost."

"Then finish packing," he said. "It's almost midnight, and you must get up before dawn."

"Don't worry. Department Chief Ch'en will come to pick me up. He has already borrowed a car."

"But you still have to get up early," he said with a reluctant smile.

"Then you...." She choked, obviously becoming emotional.

"I'm quite sleepy," he lied again, pretending to yawn.

She thought for a little while, then raised her head and said: "Well, go to sleep. Don't get up tomorrow morning when I leave. You might catch cold. You know, you're not quite well yet."

"Yes, I know." Having said this, he made a rather unsuccessful attempt to smile pleasantly at her, but when she had left the bedside to resume her packing, he shed some tears under the quilt.

Thinking that he had fallen asleep again, she continued her packing. However, he was awake all the time. His thoughts traveled to many places and to events of many years ago. They transcended the limits of time and space but kept revolving around his wife. She was still near him, but he did not dare breathe or cough lest she might be frightened away.... Looking at the wall, he cried silently until he dozed off. And that was some time after she had quietly crept into the bed.

In the small hours of the night, he woke up, drenched in cold sweat.... He wondered what time it was, then remembered that Ch'en was coming to pick up his wife. Yes. Department Chief Ch'en, a man so superior to him in every respect. He felt stupefied for several minutes.... Slowly he fell asleep again.... Looking at her sleeping husband, she decided not to wake him.... She said good-bye to him softly, and hoped that he was not dreaming of her leaving again. Still emotionally tied to her husband, she scribbled a short note and left it under the inkstand. Finally, carrying a suitcase with her, she left the room.

While Shu-sheng was going down the stairs, Hsüan suddenly awoke from a terrible dream.... The door was open and one lone suitcase stood in the middle of the room. Hastily he put on his cotton-padded gown without properly buttoning it up and carried the suitcase downstairs.

It was heavy. There was no light on the landing and the gown made him clumsy. Nevertheless, he managed to haul it down to the first floor, just as two shadows were coming up the stairs with a flashlight.

"Hsüan, you're up," a familiar voice greeted him. The flashlight shone on his face. "Oh, you've even carried my suitcase down." She walked over to him and said: "Please give it to me."

He would not release the suitcase, because he wanted to carry it down for her, insisting that he could manage it.

"Allow me," a man volunteered in a strong young voice. Hsüan was startled and immediately looked at him. He realized that the stranger was young and muscular and felt that compared to him, he himself was unworthily coarse and shabby. Obediently, he surrendered the suitcase.... Shu-sheng switched off the flashlight.

The two stood in the midst of darkness and wintry chill, listening to each other's breathing.

...She grasped his thin, hard hand. Although it was not cold, it hardly resembled that of a human being. She shuddered, suppressing her emotions and said again: "Good-bye." She was ready to leave him.

He caught her arm and cried in despair: "When shall I see you again? When will you come back?"

"I'm not sure, but I will definitely come back." ... Thus she left him.... Tears were streaming down her face.[13]

Another moving scene showing the love between mother and son occurs toward the end of the novel, when Wang's health is in a critical condition.

Mother's wish for her son's recovery was unfulfilled. Some nights later, sitting on the side of his bed, she was keeping her vigil. The dim electric light illuminated the handle of a spoon which was inside a bowl of chicken broth on a wooden bench. . . .
"Hsüan, you haven't eaten for two days. Have a little," she begged him.
Slowly, he moved his head, stretched out his hand and put his fingers in his mouth, acting as though he wanted to tear out his tongue.
"Hsüan, how do you feel? Be a little patient."
He nodded and put his hand on his throat.
"You won't die, you won't," she murmured repeatedly.
He was rubbing his throat continuously with the fingers of one hand; his movements were awkward and his fingers stiff. Suddenly his chest heaved upward.
"Hsüan, what do you want??"
He did not respond. His stiff fingers unleashed their fury, as well as they could, on his throat. His body was shaking and the wooden bed was squeaking.
"Hsüan, be patient," she repeated, pleading with him. She took his hand away from his throat, but he quickly put it back, scratching with his long fingernails and leaving bloody stripes.
"Hsüan, don't, you can't do this. . . . You can't do this. . . ," she implored him in anguish. . . .[14]

III *Dialogue*

In his use of scene, Pa Chin gives the reader a feeling of participating in the action, and he uses dialogue not only to provide the reader with a sense of immediacy and being where the action is but also to show conflicts between or among the characters. The following is an exchange of insults between Wang's mother and her daughter-in-law. Beneath the discourtesy and anger lie the sharp differences between the values of traditional and modern women.

"He's coughing so hard and yet you won't give him a moment of peace. What do you intend to do, anyway?". . .
"I plan to marry someone else. That's my intention. Are you satisfied?"
"I know your type. I know you can't take it," said Mother. . . .
"My type is not cheaper than yours," Shu-sheng responded with mounting fury.

"How dare you compare yourself to me? You're a mistress at best, and I was formally carried to the wedding in a bridal sedan-chair," said Mother very proudly.... "Everyone knows you're his mistress.... May I inquire on what date you married him? Who was the matchmaker?"...

"It's none of your business, only mine," Shu-sheng answered defiantly.

"You're my daughter-in-law, therefore it is my business. I've every right to interfere, and I intend to...," said Mother harshly.

"Let me put you straight. This is the thirty-third year of the Republic of China; it is not the reign of the Kwang-hsü or Hsüan-t'ung emperor," shouted Shu-sheng. "As for me, I never had the privilege of having my feet bound...."

"Are you mocking my bound feet? So what? No matter what, I am Hsüan's mother and therefore your elder. Don't you have any respect for age? Get out!"[15]

Another major conflict is between Wang and his wife. Their marriage is a struggle, a continuing friction, a relationship in which the wife's resentment of her husband is a persistent undercurrent. The following dialogue takes place in the fashionable International Café, where a pleading Wang tries to convince his wife to return home with him after she has moved out:

...so silent, in fact, that he finally could not endure it any longer and asked: "Are you well?"...

"Yes, I'm well," she said tersely....

"This is the first time I've been here," he remarked, not able to think of anything else to say.

"With your income you couldn't afford to come here often," she replied, pitying him with a smile.

..."I used to go to cafés, too."

"Yes, but that was eight or nine years ago. Things were different then. We have all changed a great deal in the last two years."...

"True, and who knows when these terrible days will come to an end? When we were in Shanghai, we never dreamed that we'd be as poor as we are now. We had ideals, we thought of our educational careers and wanted to establish a rural school of our own. It's strange though that our hearts should have changed so much. I don't know how or when the change began."

..."Yes, the past is like a dream. We had goals, courage, ambition.... Why can't we live like we did before?"...

"Why don't you come home with me today?"...

..."Haven't you had enough misery?"

"No, it has been all my fault," he apologized. "I don't know why I've become so temperamental."

"It's not your fault.... Who can have an even temper nowadays? I too have a quick temper."

"I think we'll have better days in the future," he said with renewed courage.

"Let's not talk about a future which is remote and far away. Life has no meaning anymore. It is a shame that with a degree in education I have to work as a junior clerk in a bank."

"What about me? I spend every day proofreading undecipherable texts. Shu-sheng, please don't talk like that. Forgive me this time and come home. I promise never to quarrel with you again," he said pleadingly....

"Don't get so agitated. Other people are staring at us," she cautioned him....[16]

IV *Monologue*

Another device used with great effectiveness is the internal monologue or "stream of consciousness." Pa Chin's type of monologue is different from that of James Joyce, Henry James, or Virginia Woolf. It is an organized monologue in which the mind presents reasoned and ordered thought, the "end-product" of the "stream of consciousness" rather than the disordered stream itself. This device is used at the very beginning of the novel. Coming out of an air-raid shelter, Wang totes up in his mind an accounting of his family life:

Maybe Hsiao-hsüan [his son] could help me.... Useless, she doesn't care for him, nor he for her. They don't seem to have any affection for each other.... What kind of family is this? Who cares for me? Everyone is for himself, and no one is willing to yield an inch.... Why am I standing here? ... Wasn't I in the shelter? Yes ... I was in it ... I feel cold ... I'm taking a walk ... I'm thinking about my quarrel with Shu-sheng. I want her home, but would she come back? I can't even find her, so how can I get her to come home?...[17]

In a similar manner, Shu-sheng asks herself what she is getting out of a life with a sickly husband: "What have I gotten from this life? Have I had any satisfaction? ... What is the price of my sacrifice? What will my life, my future be like if the situation stays like this?"[18]

A second device Pa Chin uses to reveal the thoughts of his characters is the epistolary method, which brings the reader close to the thoughts and feelings of the character. For example, in a letter Shu-sheng writes to Wang Wen-hsüan, she fully reveals her heart and mind in an analysis of her nonproductive relationship with her husband:

When I was unreasonable and angry, you always yielded to me, never saying one harsh word; you only looked entreatingly at me and did nothing. Why were you so meek? How many times have I wished that you would fight back, that you would do something ungentlemanly and turn our world upside down! Had you done so, I would have felt fulfilled; but you would only beg, sigh, and cry. When a quarrel ended, I always wanted to apologize to you, and to promise that I'd be nice to you next time. I could only pity you, but I was never able to love you. . . . [19]

A third device used to reveal a character's unconscious is the use of dreams and fantasies. Wang's feeling of insecurity about his wife's feelings toward him, his need and love for her, his love for his mother, and his apprehensions about the future are all clearly revealed in an extended dream in chapter two. Excerpts from the dream read:

. . . they were quarreling again. It was about his mother, and his wife was especially short-tempered. Angrily she overturned the dining table, breaking all the dishes. His mother was not at home, and their son hid in a corner weeping. His wife's behavior made him so tense and angry that he became speechless. He could only mutter, strike himself on the head and curse himself. . . .
. . . Suddenly the sound of cannons (so he thought) reverberated twice. . . . "The enemy is here," he told himself in alarm, and shouting "Mother" he dashed along the covered corridor toward the staircase.
"Hsüan, where are you going?" his wife called after him.
"To find my mother," he replied without turning, dashing down the stairs in one breath.
Dragging her son downstairs with her, his wife sobbed hysterically: "You can't abandon us. If we have to die, let's die together." . . .
"Let me go, I must get her. She is right here and I can't abandon her." . . .
"Okay, you go get your darling mother. I'll take Hsiao-hsüan and we'll go on our way, but don't blame me later." . . . Then she left with their son without a trace of sorrow. . . . Nonetheless he hoped that she would return to him. Maybe he could catch up with her later on. But in a flash she had vanished. He felt people crowding him from all directions, pushing and jostling, and his body was tossed to and fro like a boat in a tumultuous sea. Dazed and feverish, he pushed forward frantically with all his strength.
Then he woke up and his hands were still shaking. [20]

V Portraits of a Family: The Struggle among Mother, Son, and Daughter-in-law

A great part of the achievement of *Cold Nights* lies in Pa Chin's portraits of Wang's mother, Wang's wife, and Wang himself. Wang's mother is a widow who raised and educated her son without any help. Deeply rooted in the old traditions, she believes that a married woman should obey her husband, honor her mother-in-law, and spend most of her time at home doing housework. She sees in her daughter-in-law the living embodiment of a set of repugnant values diametrically opposed to hers. She dislikes Shu-sheng for not having insisted on a proper wedding ceremony when she married her son; she resents Shu-sheng's working at a bank and for being the one who can and does pay for her grandson's tuition; and she disapproves of Shu-sheng's dressing up "like a flower vase" and not doing much housework. In a discussion with her son about Shu-sheng's "busyness," she says with indignation: "What business is it other than going to the theater, playing Mah-Jongg or dancing? What serious business could she have? When I was a daughter-in-law, dared I ever go carousing like she does? Her son is nearly grown and she was even an education major at college."[21]

Her resentment of Shu-sheng's modern privileges barely conceals her unspoken desire to possess her son forever. Again and again, she tries to drive a wedge between her son and daughter-in-law by telling him that Shu-sheng won't stay with him and that Shu-sheng is no more than his mistress. At one point she tells him bluntly: "I can take everything except her. I'd rather die ... I don't want to see her again."[22]

For Wang, she will forever be his good mother. She is shown mending her grandson's worn-out winter jacket, washing clothes in cold weather, doing all kinds of housework, and worrying about her son's health. As he deteriorates physically from the ravages of tuberculosis, she stoops to do housework that no Chinese servant of the 1940s would touch. She scrubs, cleans, and cooks, prepares his medications for him, comforts him, and all the while hopes for his eventual recovery.

But unconsciously and simultaneously, she is also aware of the advantage to be gained from his death: he will then be hers forever. One of her great wishes has been that he remain her young and uncorrupted child, and with his death he will, in a way, fulfill her wish and make her victorious over her arch-rival, Shu-sheng.

Caught in this struggle for the only male adult in the family is Shu-sheng. Pa Chin portrays her as a good but weak-willed woman. Thirty-four years old and attractive, she enjoys patronizing cafés and going dancing with her boss, activities too costly for her sick and whining husband to afford. And when she comes home from work, she finds her dingy two-room apartment, her hostile mother-in-law, her sickly husband, and her sometimes taciturn son all too unbearable. As a "new" woman, liberated from the shackles of the past, she wants the opportunity to explore whatever blessings life may offer. Seeking to fulfill life's potential and an end to the long winter which typifies her dreary existence, she is both attracted to and repelled by her suave, rich, superior manager, Ch'en. His persistent interest in her offers both freedom and new horizon. That her dream of a better life might be satisfied by association with Ch'en and by leaving her Chungking home to go to Lanchow suggests how limited her aspirations are. Here also lies the cause of her defeat by her mother-in-law. Oscillating between inner needs and outer problems, in the end she learns that she cannot accept Manager Ch'en's love and that she really loves her husband. But by that time it is too late, for her husband has been dead and buried for more than a month. Her life can only be viewed as a failure. She fails with her husband from her own shortcomings, for (along with her half-hearted desire to possess him) she lacks the capacity and the tenacity to take on the challenges raised by her mother-in-law or to help carry the full burden of her husband's anguished soul.

Wang Wen-hsüan is the center of this struggle between the two women. His father died when he was little; as a result, he develops an attachment to his mother that colors his whole existence. Even though he loves his wife, he cannot belong to her completely while his mother lives, for as long as she is alive, he cannot really love another woman. Being torn between mother and wife debilitates him. Without the inner strength, or maybe the desire to choose one of the two, he relies on his obdurate saintliness to make living with himself possible. Willingly and knowingly, he permits, even urges, his wife to go to Lanchow, though he knows she is going to go with another man, and refuses to be a stumbling block to his wife's "pursuit of happiness." His masochism is intended to compensate for his failings as a son, for having subjected his mother to unnecessary grief; to repay her for his mostly imaginary misdeeds, he unconsciously seeks his own death. For it is only in death that he can once again be completely his mother's son, undefiled and uncomplicated by a relationship with another woman.

VI *Conclusion*

Cold Nights is a mature piece of art. In it, Pa Chin has successfully illuminated the atmosphere, the moving scenes, the interpersonal conflicts, and the inner thoughts of his characters. It is also a work of bitterness and hate — a harsh indictment of Chinese society and of the Nationalist government. He shows how an average man can be victimized by everyone, including himself. Though Pa Chin is aware of Wang Wen-hsüan's inner flaws, he still puts a large part of the blame on society and the government. With bitter irony, he describes Wang's death as occurring shortly after Japan's surrender to the Chinese: "September 3 — the Victory Day — the Day of Joy.... On that day he [Wang] thrice lost and regained consciousness. He felt that he had reached the pinnacle of man's capacity to endure; he wished that death would deliver him immediately.... When he finally expired his eyes were half shut revealing their whites and his mouth was wide open as if he were demanding justice. It was eight o'clock in the evening, and the people in the city were busy celebrating the surrender of Japan joyfully and happily amidst the sounds of countless firecrackers and displays of fireworks."[23] Pa Chin's bitterness may also be seen in his relentlessness — his refusal to mitigate pain. In great detail Pa Chin dwells on the spiritual and physical pain which lead to Wang's demise and on the events that take place within one particular family during the last year of the war. He not only makes vivid the social conditions of the time, but also enables the reader to visit with, indeed to live inside, the minds of his characters. By involving the reader in the mental and emotional experiences of its characters, *Cold Nights,* as a psychological novel, adds a significant dimension to the art of Pa Chin's prose fiction. To read such a novel is to enlarge the reader's knowledge of humanity. Herein lies the achievement of *Cold Nights.*

CHAPTER 8

Conclusion

PA Chin's life mirrors the changes in twentieth-century China. Born during the transitional period that led to the collapse of the Manchu regime and the establishment of the Republic of China, he was affected by the turmoil of the 1910s and 1920s — student agitation, new cultural impulses and movements, increased foreign aggression, and the civil strife between the Nationalists and the Communists. He suffered and lived through the long Sino-Japanese War, and welcomed the victory of the Communists in 1949. The divided country which he loved was finally united, but, ironically, under a government which denied freedom to the individual, a right which he cherished most dearly and sought to promote in his works.

In what he wrote before 1949, he was at least consistent in his artistic beliefs. From the very beginning, he was inspired by a sense of evangelical mission to do his best to help build a better society and a stronger China. He called himself a writer of conviction, and declared repeatedly that he was not an artist, that his message was more permanent than art, and that to further his convictions he would, if necessary, forsake his art without any compunction. He wrote for one purpose only — to arouse a hatred of "darkness" and a love of "light" and "truth" among his readers.

Consistent with that belief, in his early fiction he attacked what he considered to be the evils of society: capitalism, the exploitation of Chinese labor by foreigners, and other social problems. During the 1930s, his most productive period, he concentrated on one major theme: the evils in and the decline of the old family system. *Autumn in Spring* was a prelude to his most impressive achievement: the *Turbulent Stream* trilogy, the most comprehensive expatiation on the old family system yet written in modern China. *Family,* the first book of the trilogy, was well received, widely praised, and frequently compared to the classic Chinese novel *Dream of the Red Chamber* in its wide range of characters and themes. In the 1940s, he returned to his interest in the family system in *Leisure Garden* and *Cold Nights*.

During the Sino-Japanese War, like many other writers of the time, he wrote about the activities of patriots both in short stories and in the *Fire* trilogy. In *Little People, Little Things* he robbed the war of its glamour and wrote about the "little people" exactly as they were. His pessimism about China grew as the long war dragged on, and was fully reflected in *Ward Number Four* and, particularly, in *Cold Nights*.

After the Communist victory in 1949, he wrote little other than a few novels glorifying the Communist comrades in China and Korea. He seemed to have adopted a cautious attitude regarding the government, and revised many of his old works, excising parts referring to anarchism and changing the endings of many. But even such caution was not enough to protect him from attack after the Hundred Flowers period and during the Cultural Revolution. The China that he dreamed of in his youth had eluded him.

All through his life, he never wavered in his editorial mission regarding his country and his people. His writings reflect a sentimental journey from the optimism of the 1920s and 1930s to the despair of the 1940s.[1] There is no doubt that his major achievement lies in the comprehensive picture he painted of China during those twenty-odd years. It is an artist's personal record, and it correctly reflects those tumultuous years.

An ideological writer, whatever Pa Chin read became grist for his authorial mill. His reading of foreign literature, including works by Japanese, English, American, and Russian writers, helped him form his ideas. Of major importance was his exposure to anarchist and populist literature, which provided him with the political themes he used in his early works.[2] In addition, his reading gave him ideas for plots and characters. His *Snow* reminds one of Zola's *Germinal,* his *Dream on the Sea* of Turgenev's *On the Eve,* and his *Ward Number Four* of Chekhov's *Ward Number Six.* One may even detect similarities between his revolutionaries (such as Tu Ta-hsin in *Destruction* and Min in *Lightning*) and Russian populists,[3] or between Li Leng in *New Life* and Turgenev's Nezhdanov in *Virgin Soil.*[4]

Apart from reading, he also drew intellectual nourishment from what he heard from others. Whatever he heard that was useful, he incorporated into his ideological themes. For example, from the correspondence he had with one of his friends during the Château-Thierry days in 1928, he drew enough material to describe a selfish Chinese intellectual's obsession with his romantic past in chapter eight of *Destruction*.[5]

And he was obviously most interested in tales of suffering. One of his friends had spent some time in a mine in Yunnan province and had personally seen the inhumane treatment of the miners there, and thought the place a "hell on earth." Later his friend came to Shanghai and told him about his experiences in the mine. Almost immediately, the friend aroused both his sympathy and his indignation. He said: "I was compelled to pick up my pen to express the grievances of the miners. I didn't have any actual experience in mines, I wasn't even familiar with the setting or the background, and, therefore, I had to create an imaginary 'death city.' "[6] The result was a scathing attack on the industrial system.

Another very important wellspring was life as he had seen and experienced it. A realistic and imaginative observer, whatever he saw he transformed into material for his works. His acquaintance with Yuliana and a Chinese student named Wu was the source of two short stories: "Exile" and "Yali-an-na"; his visit to the mines in 1931 resulted in *Snow,* another indictment of the industrial system; his observation of the May Thirtieth Incident in 1925 inspired him to write *The Setting Sun,* a novel about striking workers; a visit to his old home in Chengtu in 1941 produced *Leisure Garden,* a novel attacking the evils money may bring; his stay at a substandard hospital in Kweiyang in 1944 materialized in the nightmarish *Ward Number Four,* which describes the grim realities of a wartime hospital; and he drew on his miserable time in Chungking, during the last year of the Sino-Japanese War, for *Cold Nights,* a harsh attack on the Nationalist government.

But his most important source of material was his own family and childhood, and his memories of them served him well. He used every scrap of childhood experience again and again, particularly in the *Turbulent Stream* trilogy. As were James Joyce, Katherine Mansfield, and Thomas Wolfe, he was self-exiled. Leaving his Chengtu home as did his hero Chüeh-hui in *Family,* he sought to find himself in France and in Shanghai and other places in China. But like many another, he found that return was just as compulsive as flight: his writing led him back to Chengtu as surely as Joyce's to Dublin, Katherine Mansfield's to the lost island of her youth, or

Thomas Wolfe's to Altamont, North Carolina. His major source of inspiration was his Chengtu home, the material from which he used again and again, elaborating, filling in, always drawing on himself and on others whom he knew intimately and well.

His ideology conditioned not only what he chose to use in his works, it also deeply affected his style of writing. He said he admired those writers who could be succinct because he could not be. With his creativity resulting from moods of "white-hot" inspiration, it is no wonder that whenever he picked up his pen it was like "having turned on the water faucet," and by the time he turned it off, "water was everywhere."[7] Because of his deep involvement with his material, he was unable to attain a sense of objectivity, and his works are usually overcharged with feeling, with heavy accumulations of grim detail; moreover, the author frequently intrudes to instruct and guide the reader.

His method, which reminds the reader of Balzac, Dreiser, and Thomas Wolfe, is perhaps neither as clumsy nor as ineffective as it appears. If his narrative method is obvious, it is by the same token never ambiguous or obscure. His own brooding presence as commentator results in a mighty singleness, a massive consistency, like the movement of a turbulent river rushing downstream. The reader is seldom simply shown anything, he is both shown and told.

Indeed, regardless of whether he used the first-person point of view, which he preferred, or the third-person point of view, Pa Chin was always the subjective omniscient commentator trying to direct the reader's thoughts. He seldom used such sophisticated techniques as limited or oblique points of view, tricks of irony or ambiguity, or narrative masks; nor did he ever tell a story in any way other than chronologically. Even when he used techniques like the extensive flashbacks often associated with stream-of-consciousness writing, he could not refrain from being an omniscient author.

When he wrote his first novel *Destruction,* he had little concept of plot, just a stomach full of emotions. Out of recollections of his childhood, he created an episodic novel which included an automobile accident and a gang of bandits robbing the poor, and stressed the protagonist's emotional nature. What he did was to string together a series of events leading to the protagonist's martyrdom. Such slipshod plot construction is to be found in many of his compositions, and even though the reader may divide his plots into "plots of fortune," "plots of action," or "plots of thought," the fact is that he paid little attention to plot construction, but merely repeated one incident or episode after another to substantiate and illustrate predetermined themes.

He always identified himself closely with his characters. Speaking of the characters in *Family,* he wrote: "The characters in the book are the same people whom I have loved and hated before. Indeed, when I wrote *Family,* it seemed as though I were suffering with those characters, struggling with them under the claws of demons and sharing with them their laughter and sorrow."[8] Consequently, his characters, in general, are reactions to his three major attitudes: love, hate, and pity. He loved his young revolutionary-martyrs and patriotic guerrilla fighters; he hated corrupt bureaucrats, factory owners, hollow intellectuals, and tyrannical family heads; and he pitied those least able to defend themselves, such as the dispossessed, the exiled, the alienated, the poor, the young, and women in general.

His themes are reflected in his gallery of stereotypes, which includes hot-headed revolutionaries, political oppressors, student radicals, hollow intellectuals, minor bureaucrats, and ordinary people. In the novels which develop the family theme, for instance, he created authoritarian elders, submissive youths, and rebels. All his characters were drawn from people whom he knew well. As a result, many of them are convincing because they have characteristics with which his readers can identify. Tu Ta-hsin in *Destruction,* Master Kao, Chüeh-hsin, Chüeh-hui, and Shu-yin in the *Turbulent Stream* trilogy, Wang Wen-hsüan, his mother, and his wife in *Cold Nights* are all memorable characters developed with considerable skill and depth.

These are the people that Pa Chin's readers knew and cared about, even though Pa Chin also pointed out the weak and venal sides of their natures. When Tu Ta-hsin says: "I cannot love, I must hate.... We were born in poverty, we die in poverty...," he is expressing the feelings of many young men of his generation who wanted to do something for their country; when Master Kao weeps silently and alone on his deathbed, the reader's sympathy is drawn to an old man who sees the passing of one generation to another; when Chüeh-hui escapes to Shanghai, when Shu-ying declares: "Spring is ours," they demonstrate by their deeds the route available to every man and woman who longs to escape from the tyranny of the family; and when two women wage war over Wang Wen-hsüan in *Cold Nights,* the reader is drawn into the tragedy that befalls a Chinese family during the trauma of World War II. Pa Chin made the reader care.

He made him care by taking him behind the scenes into the domestic privacy of his characters and by making him hear and see all that is said and done there. This enabled the reader to get inside Pa Chin's characters' minds as well as inside their houses. He alone among his contemporaries had the ability to play on the heart-strings of his reader, and the ability to gratify the sentimental urges of his time.

His characters represent universal values and yet they are individuals. Their failures and weaknesses call on the reader for the charity of his own involvement in humanity. Whether or not all his characters were developed with the same level of skill and to equal depth hardly matters; what is important is that he created so many memorable characters. Even if he had created only one Chüeh-hui, one Chüeh-hsin, or one Wang Wen-hsüan, his achievement would still have been remarkable.

In his heyday, Pa Chin was regarded as a counselor to the young; in fact, many of his works were written purposely to answer some of the personal and social problems the young faced. Since then, many of the issues he wrestled with have ceased to be of paramount interest. Unlike Lu Hsün, Mao Tun, Kuo Mo-jo, and others, Pa Chin can no longer be considered a teacher or even a creator of ferment. With the passing of time, his work can be looked on as pure art — and perhaps it has won more from this transformation than it has lost. It has perhaps taken a permanent place in the Chinese tradition, a place that stands above changes of taste or revolutions of time. We do not seek wisdom or guidance in his works, but it is impossible to imagine a time when, to a Chinese reader, *A New Life, Family, Ward Number Four,* or *Cold Nights* will cease to be among his most cherished literary pleasures.

Notes and References

Preface

1. Olga Lang, *Pa Chin and His Writings* (Cambridge: Harvard University Press, 1967), pp. 3, 275, 285, 363. See also A. Bonninger, *Etudiants chinois: Silhouettes et tendencies* (Paris, 1948), pp. 123–25.

2. *Chung-yang jih-pao (Central Daily News),* (Taipei, Taiwan), August 2, 1972.

3. Donald A. Gibbs and Yun-chen Li, *A Bibliography of Studies and Translations of Modern Chinese Literature, 1918–1942* (Cambridge: East Asian Research Center, Harvard University, 1975), pp. 150–51.

4. *Ming-pao yüeh-k'an (Ming Pao Monthly),* Vol. 10, Number 11 (November 1975), pp. 10–11.

5. Lang, p. 4.

Chapter One

1. *Pa Chin wen-chi (Collected Works of Pa Chin),* (Hong Kong: Nan-kuo ch'u-pan she, 1970), 10, *Yi (Memoirs),* p. 10. Since this is the most readily available edition in print, all references are made to this edition, unless otherwise noted. Hereafter, cited as *PCWC.*

2. *Ibid.,* p. 21. Translation by Daniel Bryant in *Sunflower Splendor,* ed. by Liu Wu-chi and Irving Y. Lo (New York, Doubleday Anchor Books, 1975), p. 301.

3. *PCWC,* 10, *Tuan-chien I (Short Notes I),* p. 16.

4. *PCWC,* 10, *Memoirs,* p. 24.

5. *Ibid.,* p. 51.

6. *PCWC,* 10, *Short Notes I,* pp. 17–18.

7. *PCWC,* 10, *Sheng chih ch'an-hui (Confessions of a Life),* p. 29.

8. *PCWC,* 10, *Memoirs,* p. 5.

9. James E. Sheridan, *China in Disintegration* (New York: The Free Press, 1975), pp. 117–21.

10. *Ibid.,* p. 121. Specifically, "May Fourth" refers to the student demonstrations in Peking in 1919. In a broad sense, "May Fourth" refers to a period of ten years, roughly from 1917–1927.

11. *PCWC,* 10, *Memoirs,* p. 71.

12. Roger N. Baldwin, ed., *Kropotkin's Revolutionary Pamphlets* (New York: Dover Publications, 1970), p. 260.

13. *PCWC*, 10, *Short Notes I,* pp. 7–8.

14. *Ibid.,* p. 8.

15. *Ibid.,* p. 9.

16. *Ibid.,* pp. 10–11.

17. *PCWC*, 10, *Memoirs,* p. 66.

18. George Woodcock and Ivan Avakumovic, *The Anarchist Prince: A Biographical Study of Peter Kropotkin* (New York: Kraus Reprint, 1970), p. 26.

19. *PCWC*, 10, *Memoirs,* pp. 72–77.

20. *PCWC*, 10, *Short Notes I,* p. 20.

21. *PCWC*, 10, *Memoirs,* p. 68.

22. *Ibid.,* p. 69.

23. *PCWC*, 10, *Short Notes I,* p. 20.

24. *PCWC*, 10, *Memoirs,* p. 70.

25. Sheridan, pp. 152–53.

26. *PCWC*, 11, *Hai-hsing tsa-chi (Sea Voyage Notebook),* pp. 8–9.

27. *PCWC*, 7, "Hsieh-tso sheng-huo ti hui-ku" ("Recollections of a Writer's Life"), p. 2.

28. *Ibid.,* pp. 2–4.

29. Olga Lang, p. 7. " 'Pa' stands for the first syllable of the name Bakunin, and 'Chin' for the last syllable of the name Kropotkin (Pa-k'u-ning and K'o-lu-p'ao-t'e-chin respectively in Chinese transcription)." However, in the Epilogue Lang says, on pp. 269–70: "Pa Chin now denies even the origin of his pen name. 'Pa' has nothing to do with Bakunin but it is the name of a Chinese student who lived for one month in the students' dormitory in Château-Thierry (and later committed suicide); 'Chin' still stands for the last syllable of Kropotkin's name but it came into our writer's name almost accidentally: a friend who knew that he was looking for a suitable pen name and saw Kropotkin's book on his desk 'half-jokingly' suggested that 'Chin' would be a good second part of that name."

30. *PCWC*, 14, *T'an tzu-chi ti ch'uang-tso (Discussion of My Creative Work),* p. 5. Hereafter, *Discussion.*

31. Sheridan, pp. 183–84.

32. *PCWC*, 10, *Memoirs,* pp. 87–88.

33. *Ibid.,* p. 89.

34. Lang, p. 249. Lang compared *Snow* to Zola's *Germinal* and regarded both works as fascinating.

35. *PCWC*, 11, *Lü-t'u sui-pi (Random Voyage Notes),* pp. 8–9.

36. *PCWC*, 2, *Sha-ting (The Antimony Miners),* pp. 3–4.

37. *PCWC*, 10, *Confessions of a Life,* pp. 39–44.

38. *PCWC*, 11, *Random Voyage Notes,* p. 97.

39. *PCWC*, 7, "Recollections of a Writer's Life," p. 8.

40. *PCWC*, 10, *Memoirs,* p. 104.

41. *PCWC*, 7, *Kuang-ming (Light),* p. 10.

42. PCWC, 10, *Memoirs,* p. 104.

43. *PCWC,* 10, *Confessions of a Life,* p. 37. See also *PCWC,* 10, *Tien-ti (Drops),* p. 23.

44. *PCWC,* 10, *Drops,* p. 26.

45. *PCWC,* 10, *Wu-t'i (No Title),* p. 62.

46. *PCWC,* 10, *K'ung-su (J'Accuse),* pp. 22–23.

47. *PCWC,* 11, *Lü-t'u t'ung-hsün (Letters on the Road),* pp. 10–11.

48. *Ibid.,* p. 13.

49. *PCWC,* 10, *Huai-nien (Reminiscences),* p. 3.

50. *PCWC,* 10, *Ching-yeh ti pei-shü (Tragedy on a Quiet Night),* pp. 81–82.

51. *PCWC,* 10, *Reminiscences,* p. 61.

52. *Ibid.,* pp. 62–63.

53. Chen Tan-chen, "Pa Chin the Novelist," *Chinese Literature,* No. 6 (Peking, 1963), pp. 84–92.

54. Hsu Kai-yu, *The Chinese Literary Scene* (New York: Vintage Books, 1975), p. 24.

55. Merle Goldman, *Literary Dissent in Communist China* (Cambridge: Harvard University Press, 1967), p. 244.

56. C. T. Hsia, *A History of Modern Chinese Fiction* (New Haven and London: Yale University Press, 1961), p. 640; see also Goldman, p. 263.

57. *PCWC,* 14, *Discussion,* p. 18.

58. *Ibid.,* p. 34.

59. *Ibid.,* pp. 36–37.

60. *PCWC,* 10, *Short Notes I,* pp. 12–13.

61. Olga Lang, ed., *Family* (New York: Doubleday Anchor Books, 1972), p. xxv.

62. *Central Daily News,* July 27, 1977.

Chapter Two

1. Hsu Kai-yu, *Twentieth Century Chinese Poetry* (Ithaca: Cornell University Press, 1970), pp. xvi–xvii.

2. Wang Yao, *Chung-kuo hsin wen-hsüeh shih-kao (A Draft History of Modern Chinese Literature)* (Shanghai: Hsin wen-yi she, 1954), Vol. 1, p. 54.

3. *Ibid.*

4. Walter J. Meserve and Ruth I. Meserve, eds., *Modern Literature From China* (New York: New York University Press, 1974), pp. 1–2.

5. *PCWC,* 14, *Discussion,* p. 5.

6. Chow Tse-tsung, *The May Fourth Movement: Intellectual Revolution in Modern China* (Cambridge: Harvard University Press, 1960), p. 287.

7. *PCWC,* 7, *Tien-yi (The Electric Chair),* p. 9. See also Hsiao Ch'ien, *Etchings of a Tormented Age* (London: George Allen & Unwin, 1942), p. 19.

8. *PCWC*, 3, *Ai-ch'ing ti san-pu-ch'ü (The Love Trilogy)*, pp. 533–34.

9. *PCWC*, 14, *Discussion*, pp. 60–61.

10. *PCWC*, 12, *Huo I (Fire I)*, p. 177. Translation by C. T. Hsia in *History*, p. 376.

11. Mark Schorer, "Technique As Discovery," in Philip Stevik, ed., *The Theory of the Novel* (New York: The Free Press, 1967), p. 71.

12. *Ibid.*, p. 67.

13. *PCWC*, 1, *Mieh-wang (Destruction)*, p. 45.

14. *Ibid.*, p. 59.

15. *Ibid.*, pp. 97–98.

16. *Ibid.*, pp. 99–100.

17. *Ibid.*, p. 1.

18. *Ibid.*, p. 135.

19. *PCWC*, 1, *Hsin-sheng (New Life)*, pp. 9–10.

20. *Ibid.*, p. 12.

21. *Ibid.*, p. 14.

22. *Ibid.*, p. 30.

23. *Ibid.*, p. 42.

24. *Ibid.*, p. 64.

25. *Ibid.*, p. 61.

26. *Ibid.*, p. 165.

27. *Ibid.*, p. 169.

28. Olga Lang, *Pa Chin and His Writings*, p. 142.

29. *PCWC*, 3, *Wu (Fog)*, p. 42.

30. *Ibid.*, p. 43.

31. *Ibid.*, pp. 97–98.

32. *PCWC*, 1, *Destruction*, p. 99.

33. *PCWC*, 3, *Yü (Rain)*, p. 282.

34. *Pa Chin and His Writings*, p. 245.

35. *PCWC*, 3, *Tien (Lightning)*, p. 424.

36. *PCWC*, 3, *Fog*, p. 56.

37. *Ibid.*, p. 89.

38. Hsia, *History*, pp. 262–63.

39. In his story, "Ya-li-an-na," Pa Chin describes Yuliana's attitude toward free love and her love affair with a Chinese student; in "Mei-kuei hua ti hsiang" ("The Fragrance of Roses") he portrays a young woman who, in the embrace of her lover, mutters: "This moment, let it last forever. . . . Let love chase everything away" (*PCWC*, 8, *Chiang-chün* [*The General*], p. 120).

40. *PCWC*, 3, *Lei (Thunder)*, p. 306.

41. *PCWC*, 2, *Ch'un-t'ien li ti ch'iu-t'ien (Autumn in Spring)*, p. 77.

42. *Ibid.*, p. 15.

43. Mary Wright, ed., *China in Revolution, The First Phase 1900–1913* (New Haven: Yale University Press, 1968), p. 234.

44. Mary Backus Rankin, *Early Chinese Revolutionaries. Radical Intel-*

lectuals in Shanghai and Chekiang, 1902–1911 (Cambridge: Harvard University Press, 1971), p. 27.

45. *PCWC*, 1, *Ssu-ch'ü ti t'ai-yang (The Setting Sun)*, p. 32. The novel also includes two other themes: romance and industrial blight. The love element is slight. Following Pa Chin's shop-worn formula of parents tearing lovers asunder, student Wu Yang-ch'ing's love affair with Miss Ch'en Ching-feng leads inevitably to Miss Ch'en's dying of a broken heart. Yet, in his treatment of industrial blight, Pa Chin suggests that while students often debate issues, it is the workers who suffer. In fact, the strikers of Yi-chi factory in Nanking suffer so much that one worker's daughter literally dies of starvation. This worker, Li A-ken, then sets fire to the Yi-chi factory building. His collaborator, Wang Hsüeh-li, a union leader, is later executed by the authorities. Pa Chin's conclusion seems to be that what the workers need is food, not inflammatory speeches.

46. *Ibid.*, pp. 8–9.

47. *Ibid.*, p. 107.

48. *PCWC*, 2, *The Antimony Miners*, p. 16.

49. Gerald Runkle, ed., *Anarchism Old and New* (New York: Delacorte Press, 1972), p. 80.

50. *PCWC*, 2, *The Antimony Miners*, p. 79.

51. *PCWC*, 2, *Hsüeh (Snow)*, p. 18.

52. *Pa Chin and His Writings*, p. 124.

53. Tu Ta-hsin's poem on the fate of a peasant in the hands of bandits includes the following lines: "In a weak and anguished voice, he unceasingly pleads: / 'Masters, kind masters, spare my dog-life, one not worth a penny. Spare me. / May the heavens bless you all — bless you all with good fortunes.' / In such a thread-like manner the hopeless cries of a dying dog / Fail to persuade the bandits to drop their sharp knives. / ...Knives are smeared with blood. / The ground is dyed in fresh blood. / Hands are filled with fresh blood...." (*PCWC*, 1, *Destruction*, pp. 15–16).

54. Runkle, p. 110.

55. Paul Avrich, *The Russian Anarchists* (Princeton: Princeton University Press, 1967), p. 97.

56. Martin A. Miller, ed., *Selected Writings on Anarchism and Revolution by Peter A. Kropotkin* (Cambridge: The MIT Press, 1970), p. 20.

Chapter Three

1. See "T'an wo-ti tuan-p'ien hsiao-shuo" ("Discussion of My Short Stories") and "T'an wo-ti san-wen" ("Discussion of My Essays") in *PCWC*, 14, *Discussion*, pp. 151–78.

2. *PCWC*, 8, *The General*, p. 96.

3. *Ibid.*, p. 97.

4. Ibid., p. 104.

5. *Ibid.,* p. 106.

6. *Ibid.,* p. 8.

7. *Ibid.,* p. 192.

8. *Ibid.*

9. *PCWC,* 7, *Light,* p. 53.

10. *Ibid.,* p. 59.

11. *Ibid.,* p. 62. In the 1940 edition published by the K'ai-ming Bookstore of Shanghai, the ending reads as follows: "I thought also that an armless but fair and just Immortal still sat in that lonely temple, yet I would never be able to kneel before the altar and pray."

12. *PCWC,* 8, *The General,* p. 80.

13. Rankin, p. 1.

14. T. S. Eliot, *The Complete Poems and Plays 1909-1950* (New York: Harcourt, Brace and World, 1962), p. 56.

15. *PCWC,* 8, *Ch'en-lo (Sinking Down),* p. 65.

16. *Ibid.,* pp. 64-65.

17. Eliot, p. 56.

18. *PCWC,* 8, *Sinking Down,* p. 79.

19. *PCWC,* 8, *Shen, kuei, jen (God, Ghost, Man),* p. 49.

20. *PCWC,* 9, *Ch'ang-sheng t'a (Pagoda of Long Life),* pp. 3-4.

21. *Ibid.,* p. 5.

22. *Ibid.,* p. 41.

23. *Ibid.,* p. 65.

24. One of the typical prefaces is the one to *Fu-ch'ou (Revenge)* in *PCWC,* 7, pp. 17-18.

25. *PCWC,* 7, *Revenge,* p. 23.

26. *Ibid.,* p. 24.

27. *Ibid.,* pp. 29-30.

28. *Ibid.,* p. 47. Translation by Diana Beverly Granat in "Three Stories of France: Pa Chin and His Early Short Stories," 1972 University of Pennsylvania Master's Thesis, p. 56.

29. *PCWC,* 7, *Revenge,* p. 50.

30. *Ibid.,* pp. 54-55; Granat, pp. 66-68, with slight changes.

31. *PCWC,* 7, *Revenge,* p. 56; Granat, pp. 69-71, with slight changes.

32. *PCWC,* 7, *Light,* p. 33.

33. *Ibid.,* p. 63; Granat, p. 84.

34. *PCWC,* 7, *Light,* p. 66; Granat, p. 76.

35. *PCWC,* 7, *Light,* p. 71; Granat, pp. 83-84.

36. *PCWC,* 7, *The Electric Chair,* p. 109.

37. *Ibid.,* pp. 120-21.

38. *PCWC,* 7, *Revenge,* p. 58. Translation by Mo Chin-yin in *Short Stories by Pa Chin, with English Translations* (Hong Kong: Hui-t'ung shu-tien, 1963), p. 2.

39. *PCWC,* 7, *Revenge,* p. 68.

40. *Ibid.*

41. *Ibid.*

42. *Ibid.,* pp. 39–40; Granat, pp. 42–45, with slight changes.

43. *PCWC,* 7, *Revenge,* pp. 41–42; Granat, p. 47.

44. *PCWC,* 7, *Revenge,* p. 46; Granat, pp. 54–55.

Chapter Four

1. Chow Tse-tsung, p. 73.

2. *Ibid.,* p. 1.

3. C. K. Yang, *The Chinese Family in the Communist Revolution* (Cambridge: The MIT Press, 1959), p. 9.

4. *Ibid.,* p. 12.

5. *Ibid.,* p. 13.

6. See Pa Chin's "To a Cousin — Preface to the 10th Edition of *Family*" tr. by Shang-lan Mui Yeh in *Renditions,* Number 4, (Spring 1975), p. 77.

7. *Ibid.*

8. Oldrich Král, "Pa Chin's Novel *The Family,*" in *Studies in Modern Chinese Literature,* ed. by J. Provek (Berlin: Akademie-Verlag, 1964), p. 110.

9. *PCWC,* 5, *Ch'un (Spring),* p. 535.

10. See *Pa Chin and His Writings,* p. 197; see also Ts'ao Chü-jen, *Wen-t'an wu-shih-nien hsü chi (Fifty Years of the World of Letters, Continued)* (Hong Kong: Hsin wen-hu ch'u-pan she, 1969), pp. 39–40.

11. *PCWC,* 4, *Chia (Family),* pp. 107–108. Translation by Sidney Shapiro in *The Family* (Peking: Foreign Languages Press, 1964), pp. 87–88. Shapiro's translation contains many omissions which have been restored.

12. *PCWC,* 4, *Family,* p. 119; Shapiro, p. 97.

13. *PCWC,* 4, *Family,* pp. 397–98; Shapiro, 282–84.

14. *PCWC,* 4, *Family,* p. 8.

15. A woman's three obediences are to obey her father, her husband, and later her son; her four virtues are right behavior, proper speech, proper demeanor, and proper employment.

16. *PCWC,* 4, *Family,* pp. 381–82; Shapiro, pp. 270–71.

17. *PCWC,* 6, *Ch'iu (Autumn),* p. 265.

18. *PCWC,* 4, *Family,* p. 403; Shapiro, p. 286.

19. *PCWC,* 6, *Autumn,* pp. 668–69. Translation by Betty Wong in "Pa Chin in His Middle Period as a Novelist: An Analysis of Characters in the *Torrent Trilogy* and *Fire,*" Master's Thesis, Columbia University, 1967, pp. 121–22, with substantive changes.

20. *The Hsiao Ching,* tr. by Mary Leila Makra (New York: St. John's University Press, 1961), p. 23.

21. *PCWC,* 4, *Family,* p. 130; Shapiro, p. 104.

22. *PCWC,* 4, *Family,* p. 152; Shapiro, p. 121.

23. *PCWC,* 4, *Family,* pp. 387–88; Shapiro, pp. 275–76.

24. *PCWC,* 5, *Autumn,* p. 333.

25. *Ibid.,* p. 533.

26. Cleanth Brooks and Robert Penn Warren, *Understanding Fiction,* 2nd Edition (New York: Appleton Century Crofts, 1959), pp. 687, 183.

27. Leo Ou-fan Lee, *The Romantic Generation of Modern Chinese Writers* (Cambridge: Harvard University Press, 1973), p. 263.

28. Lin Yutang, *The Importance of Living* (New York: The John Day Company, 1937), pp. 434–35.

29. Leo Lee, p. 265.

30. *Ibid.,* p. 196.

31. *PCWC,* 4, *Family,* p. 219; Shapiro, p. 171.

32. *PCWC,* 4, *Family,* p. 219; Shapiro, p. 171.

33. *PCWC,* 4, *Family,* p. 215; Shapiro, p. 167.

34. *PCWC,* 4, *Family,* p. 154; Shapiro, pp. 122–23.

35. *PCWC,* 4, *Family,* p. 115; Shapiro, p. 95.

36. *PCWC,* 4, *Family,* p. 444; Shapiro, p. 315.

37. *PCWC,* 4, *Family,* p. 217; Shapiro, p. 169.

38. *PCWC,* 4, *Family,* p. 115; Shapiro, p. 95.

39. *PCWC,* 4, *Family,* p. 366; Shapiro, pp. 258–59.

40. *PCWC,* 4, *Family,* pp. 276–80; Shapiro, pp. 205–208, with slight changes.

41. *PCWC,* 4, *Family,* pp. 420–21; Shapiro, 300–301, with slight changes.

42. *PCWC,* 6, *Autumn,* p. 578; Betty Wong, p. 56.

43. *PCWC,* 6, *Autumn,* p. 580; Betty Wong, p. 57.

Chapter Five

1. Sheridan, pp. 243–44.

2. Howard Goldblatt, *Hsiao Hung* (Boston: Twayne Publishers, 1976), p. 61.

3. Wang Yao, Vol. 2, p. 3.

4. Hsia, *History,* p. 315.

5. Wang Yao, Vol. 2, p. 86.

6. *PCWC,* 9, *Huan-hun ts'ao (The Grass of Resurrection),* p. 9.

7. *PCWC,* 12, *Huo 1 (Fire 1),* p. 177. Translation by Hsia in *History,* p. 376.

8. *PCWC,* 12, *Fire 2,* p. 334.

9. See the 1945 Chungking K'ai-ming edition of *Fire 3.*

10. *PCWC,* 12, *Fire 3,* p. 447.

11. *Pa Chin and His Writings,* p. 209.

12. Quoted in Hsia's *History,* p. 377.

13. *Ibid.*

14. *PCWC,* 9, *Hsiao-jen, hsiao-shih (Little People, Little Things),* p. 28.

15. *Ibid.,* p. 38.

16. *Ibid.,* p. 40.

17. *Ibid.,* p. 56.

18. *Ibid.,* p. 20.

19. *Ibid.,* p. 36.

20. *Ibid.,* p. 53.

21. *PCWC,* 13, *Ti-ssu ping-shih (Ward Number Four),* p. 6.

22. *Ibid.,* p. 96.

23. *Ibid.,* p. 179.

24. *Ibid.*

25. The squalid hospital, the suffering patients, the callous janitor, and the title of the book readily remind one of Chekhov's *Ward Number Six.* But the two are identical in only one aspect: Lao Ch'eng, the janitor in *Ward Number Four,* and Nikita in *Ward Number Six* both contribute to the sufferings of the patients. *Ward Number Four* is a surgical ward, while *Ward Number Six* is a mental ward. Patients in the former are confined to their beds most of the time, while those in the latter have some measure of freedom in walking from window to window. In both, admittedly, emaciated patients sing softly or sometimes display childish gaiety, mourn, sigh, and lament. In both, they eat and drink mechanically. But there are differences between the two novels. *Ward Number Four* describes the generally squalid condition of the ward while *Ward Number Six* centers on the debate between two characters, Ivan Dmitrich, a patient suffering from the mania of persecution, and Dr. Ragin. The relationship between the narrator and Dr. Yang in *Ward Number Four* nowhere matches the intensity between that of Ivan Dmitrich and Dr. Ragin. While the narrator in *Ward Number Four* is a childish young adult who adores Dr. Yang, Ivan, though also young, is well versed in philosophy. He is not impressed by Dr. Ragin's quotations from Marcus Aurelius and questions Ragin's right to preach such a gospel. Pa Chin's Dr. Yang speaks of the war, home, family, and recites T'ang poetry, while Dr. Ragin speaks of the philosophy of nonresistance, of his clear conscience in standing aside from the problems of life. Perhaps the most significant difference is that Dr. Yang later leaves the hospital and works valiantly to save the lives of war victims, while Dr. Ragin dies of an apoplectic fit in the hospital with all his theories of passivity and indifference completely overthrown.

Chapter Six

1. See "T'an *Ch'i-yüan*" ("Discussion of *Leisure Garden*") in *PCWC,* 14, p. 109. Pa Chin wrote: "During my two visits to Szechwan in January, 1941, and in May, 1942, I saw the might of money ... Chengtu

was a paradise for parasites and exploiters, breeding many different types of people who did not work but who profited from their wealth. The rich landowners could not spend all their rentals and accumulated more land. . . . They hid in their houses, and, using the services of 'deputies,' lived on exploitation.''

2. *PCWC,* 13, *Ch'i-yüan (Leisure Garden),* p. 9.
3. *Ibid.,* p. 109.
4. *Ibid.*
5. *PCWC,* 14, *Discussion,* p. 117.
6. *PCWC,* 13, *Leisure Garden,* pp. 122–23.
7. *Ibid.,* p. 128.
8. *Ibid.,* p. 108.
9. *Ibid.,* p. 113.
10. *Ibid.,* p. 115.
11. *Ibid.,* p. 93.
12. *Ibid.,* p. 3.
13. *Ibid.,* p. 43.
14. *Ibid.,* p. 44.
15. *Ibid.,* p. 66.
16. Hsia, *History,* p. 378.

Chapter Seven

1. *PCWC,* 14, *Han-yeh (Cold Nights),* pp. 295–96. In the postscript Pa Chin writes: ''In the winter of 1944, when Kweilin fell to the Japanese, I lived in a tiny room below the Culture and Life office on Ming-kuo Road in Chungking. At night I frequently had to use a candle for light and at midnight had to use my thermos jug to carry the hot water I bought to drink from an old hawker selling 'fried rice-cakes and hot water.' I usually slept late, and the scurrying rats digging holes in the floor disturbed my sleep. During the day, the noises of hawkers, quarrels, talking, and of the gong and drum from a nearby theater intruded into my room and deprived me, enclosed as I was in a tiny cell, of any quiet. At that time I was proofreading the translation of a novel by Gorki and sometimes I did a few favors for my refugee friends from Kweilin. One day Mr. Chao Chia-pi came to see me at the Culture and Life office. He was penniless. His career in Kweilin had been destroyed by the enemy's firepower. . . . Then one winter night I began to write my long novel *Han-yeh.* I was never a great writer, but I had never dared to write an epic. As one critic pointed out I 'dared not face the bloody realities of life,' so using tidbits of what I knew and had heard, I wrote about the blood-tinged phlegm of a tuberculosis victim, the life and death of an insignificant but educated man. I did not lie. I saw his blood-tinged phlegm which remains fresh in my mind. The phlegm forced me to speak out for all those dead who had to spit out their phlegm and those who had not. With frequent interruptions I com-

pleted the novel after two years. . . . In the interim victory had come bringing us hope which soon dissipated into thin air.''

2. *Ihid.*, p. 294.
3. *Ibid.*, p. 5.
4. *Ibid.*, pp. 9, 12.
5. *Ibid.*, p. 205.
6. *Ibid.*, p. 172.
7. *Ibid.*, p. 103.
8. *Ibid.*
9. *Ibid.*, p. 286.
10. *Ibid.*, p. 294.
11. *Ibid.*, p. 110.
12. *Ibid.*, p. 106.
13. *Ibid.*, pp. 211–16.
14. *Ibid.*, pp. 280–81.
15. *Ibid.*, pp. 158–60.
16. *Ibid.*, pp. 30–32.
17. *Ibid.*, pp. 7–8.
18. *Ibid.*, p. 161.
19. *Ibid.*, pp. 235–36.
20. *Ibid.*, pp. 14–17.
21. *Ibid.*, p. 65.
22. *Ibid.*, p. 152.
23. *Ibid.*, pp. 284–85.

Chapter Eight

1. See Nathan Mao, ''Pa Chin's Journey in Sentiment: From Hope to Despair,'' *Journal of the Chinese Language Teachers Association,* Vol. XI, No. 2 (May 1976), pp. 131–37.
2. *Pa Chin and His Writings,* pp. 224–30.
3. *Ibid.*, p. 240.
4. *Ibid.*, p. 241.
5. *PCWC,* 7, ''Recollections of a Writer's Life,'' p. 5.
6. *PCWC,* 14, *Discussion,* p. 40.
7. *Ibid.*, p. 3.
8. *Ibid.*, p. 44.

Selected Bibliography

PRIMARY SOURCES

(This list does not include Pa Chin's collected essays and translations. A detailed list is given in Olga Lang's *Pa Chin and His Writings,* pp. 341–53.)

Pa Chin hsüan-chi (Pa Chin's Selected Works). Shanghai: Chung-yang shu-tien, 1936.

Pa Chin hsüan-chi (Pa Chin's Selected Works). Peking: K'ai-ming, 1951.

Pa Chin san-wen hsüan (Pa Chin's Selected Essays). Peking: Hsin-hua, 1955.

Pa Chin tai-piao-tso hsüan (Selections of Representative Works of Pa Chin). Shanghai: Ch'üan ch'ui, 1951.

Pa Chin wen-chi (Collected Works of Pa Chin), 14 volumes. Peking: Jen-min wen-hsüeh, 1958–1962.

Pa Chin wen-chi (Collected Works of Pa Chin), 14 volumes. Hong Kong: Nan-kuo ch'u-pan she, 1970. This is the most accessible edition. Texts differ slightly from the pre-1951 editions. Vol. 1: *Mieh-wang (Destruction,* 1927–1928); *Hsin-sheng (New Life,* 1931, 1932); *Ssu-ch'ü ti t'ai-yang (The Setting Sun,* 1930); and *Hai ti meng (Dream on the Sea,* 1932); Vol. 2: *Ch'un-t'ien li ti ch'iu-t'ien (Autumn in Spring,* 1932); *Sha-ting (The Antimony Miners,* 1932); *Hsüeh (Snow,* 1933); *Li-na (Lina,* 1934); Vol. 3: *Wu (Fog,* 1931); *Yü (Rain,* 1932), *Lei (Thunder,* 1933); *Tien (Lightning,* 1934); Vol. 4: *Chia (Family,* 1931); Vol. 5: *Ch'un (Spring,* 1938); Vol. 6: *Ch'iu (Autumn,* 1940); Vol. 7: *Fu-ch'ou (Revenge,* 1929–1931); *Kuang-ming (Light,* 1931); *Tien-yi (The Electric Chair,* 1931–1932); Vol. 8: *Mo-pu (The Dustcloth,* 1931–1932); *Chiang-chün (The General,* 1932–1933); *Ch'en-mo (Deep Silence,* 1934); *Ch'en-lo (Sinking Down,* 1934); *Shen, kuei, jen (God, Ghost, Man,* 1934–1935); Vol. 9: *Ch'en-mo II (Deep Silence II,* 1934); *Fa ti ku-shih (Story of Hair,* 1936); *Ch'ang-sheng t'a (Pagoda of Long Life,* 1934–1936); *Huan-hun ts'ao (Grass of Resurrection,* 1937–1941); *Hsiao-jen, hsiao-shih (Little People, Little Things,* 1942–1945); Vol. 10: *Yi (Memoirs,* 1933–1936); *Tuan-chien I (Short Notes I,* 1936); *Sheng chih ch'an-hui (Confessions of a Life,* 1929–1934); *Tien-ti (Drops,* 1934–1935); *Meng yü tsui (Dream and Inebriation,* 1937); *K'ung-su (J'Accuse,* 1931–1937); *Wu-t'i (No Title,*

1936–1940); *Hei-t'u* (*Black Earth,* 1939); *Lung, hu, kou* (*Dragon, Tiger, Dog,* 1940–1941); *Fei-yüan wai* (*Behind a Desolate Garden,* 1938–1942); *Hui-nien* (*Reminiscences,* 1938–1946); *Ching-yeh ti pei-chü* (*Tragedy on a Quiet Night,* 1945–1946); Vol. 11: *Hai-hsing tsa-chi* (*Sea Voyage Notebook,* 1927); *Lü-t'u sui-pi* (*Random Notes of a Voyage,* 1933–1934); *Lü-t'u t'ung-hsün* (*Letters on the Road,* 1938–1939); *Lü-t'u tsa-chi* (*Travel Noebook,* 1940–1942); *Tuan-chien II* (*Short Notes II,* 1935–1937); Vol. 12: *Huo* (*Fire,* 1938–1940, 1941, 1943); Vol. 13: *Ch'i-yüan* (*Leisure Garden,* 1944); *Ti-ssu ping-shih* (*Ward Number Four,* 1945); Vol. 14: *Han-yeh* (*Cold Nights,* 1946); *T'an tzu-chi ti ch'ung-tso* (*Discussion of My Creative Work,* 1957–1961).

A Battle for Life: A Full Record of How the Life of Steel Worker Chiu Tsai-kang Was Saved in the Shanghai Kwangtze Hospital (*I-ch'ang wan-chiu sheng-ming ti chan-tou*). Pa Chin et al. Tr. by Cheng Chih-yi and Shen Tzu-kao. Peking: Foreign Languages Press, 1959.

Li Ta-hai. Peking: Tso-chia ch'u-pan she, 1961.

Living Amongst Heroes. Peking: Foreign Languages Press, 1954.

Lo-ch'e shang (On the Mule Cart). Hong Kong: Hsin-yüeh Publishing Company, 1959.

Ming-chu ho Yü-chi (Ming-chu and Yü-chi). Peking: Chung-kuo shao-nien erh-t'ung ch'u-pan she, 1957.

Wo-men hui-chien liao P'eng Te-huai Ssu-ling yüan (Our Meeting with Commander P'eng Te-huai). Peking: Wen-hsüeh ch'u-pan she, 1953.

Ying-hsiung ti ku-shih (Stories of Heroes). Shanghai: P'ing-ming ch'u-pan she, 1953.

SECONDARY SOURCES

ANONYMOUS. "The Collected Works of Pa Chin." *Chinese Literature,* 1953. No. 4, pp. 117–20. Introduces Pa Chin's collected works (in 14 vols).

AVRICH, PAUL. *The Russian Anarchists.* Princeton: Princeton University Press, 1967. Important to the study of Russian anarchists. Includes a useful chronology of events from 1876 through 1964 and an annotated bibliography.

BENEDIKTER, MARTIN. "Un Racconto di Pa Chin: Cane," in *Cina* 6. Rome: Instituto italiana per il Medio ed Estremo Oriente, 1960, pp. 88–89. Brief note on Pa Chin.

BOORMAN, HOWARD C., and HOWARD, RICHARD C., eds. *Biographical Dictionary of Republican China.* 4 volumes. New York: Columbia University Press, 1967–1971. Vol. 2, pp. 297–99; Vol. 4, pp. 249–52. Useful as a general reference.

BRIERE, O. "Un Romancier Chinois Contemporarin: Pa Chin," in *Bulletin de l'Universite l'Aurore.* Shanghai: Serie 3, 3.3 (1942), pp. 577–98. One of the earliest studies on Pa Chin.

CHANG, TANG, tr. "Perseverance" ("Chien ch'iang chan-shih") in *Chinese Literature,* 1963, No. 6, pp. 47–62.

CHEN TAN-CHEN. "Pa Chin the Novelist" in *Chinese Literature,* 1963, No. 6, pp. 84–92. Discusses Pa Chin's life and work after 1949.

CHOW TSE-TSUNG. *The May Fourth Movement: Intellectual Revolution in Modern China.* Cambridge: Harvard University Press, 1960. Remains the most authoritative book on the subject.

Chung-yang jih-pao (Central Daily News). Taiwan: Taipei. August 2, 1972. Contains an anonymous article on the revival of interest in Pa Chin's works in Mainland China.

_____. Taiwan, Taipei. July 27, 1977. Contains an anonymous article on Pa Chin's persecution by the Gang of Four.

GIBBS, DONALD A., and LI, YUN-CHEN. *A Bibliography of Studies and Translations of Modern Chinese Literature, 1918–1942.* Cambridge: Harvard East Asian Research Center, 1975. Useful general reference book. Contains a section on Pa Chin, pp. 150–54.

GOLDBLATT, HOWARD. *Hsiao Hung.* Boston: Twayne Publishers, 1976. An interpretive study of Hsiao Hung's life and work. Well written.

GOLDMAN, MERLE. *Literary Dissent in Communist China.* Cambridge: Harvard University Press, 1967. Scholarly and well documented.

_____, ed. *Modern Chinese Literature in the May Fourth Era.* Cambridge: Harvard University Press, 1977. Contains seventeen critical essays on the study of modern Chinese literature.

GRANAT, DIANA. "Three Stories of France: Pa Chin and His Early Short Stories." Unpublished M.A. Thesis. University of Pennsylvania, 1972. Introduction too sketchy, but the translations of "Fang-tung t'ai-t'ai" ("Mrs. Landlady"), "Lo-po-erh hsien-sheng" ("M. Robert"), and "Hao-jen" ("A Good Man") are useful.

GRIEDER, JEROME. *Hu Shih and the Chinese Renaissance.* Cambridge: Harvard University Press, 1970. Excellent study.

HOWE, IRVING. *Politics and the Novel.* New York: Avon Books, 1967. Studies the impact of ideology on writers.

HSIA, C. T. *A History of Modern Chinese Fiction.* New Haven and London: Yale University Press, 1961. The best general survey of twentieth-century Chinese fiction.

HSIA, T. A. *The Gate of Darkness: Studies on the Leftist Literary Movement in China.* Seattle: University of Washington Press, 1968. Contains six essays on six modern Chinese writers.

HSIAO CH'IEN. *Etchings of a Tormented Age.* London: George Allen & Unwin Company, 1942. Concise and easy to read.

HSU, KAI-YU. *The Chinese Literary Scene.* New York: Vintage, 1975. Chatty and interesting.

_____. *Twentieth Century Chinese Poetry.* Ithaca: Cornell University Press, 1976. Contains a good introduction to and selections of twentieth-century Chinese poetry.

JEN, RICHARD L., tr. "Star" ("Hsing") in *T'ien Hsia Monthly*, 5.1 (August 1937), pp. 68–78; 5.2 (September 1937), pp. 193–207; 5.3 (October 1937), pp. 313–25; 5.4 (November 1937), pp. 404–14. Reprinted as *Star*. Shanghai: Shih-chiah ying-yü pien-yi she, 1947. No longer available.

KALMER, J., tr. *Garten der Ruhe (Leisure Garden)*. Munich: G. Kauser, 1954.

KRÁL, OLDŘICH. "Pa Chin's Novel 'The Family' " in Jaroslav Provek, ed. *Studies in Modern Chinese Literature*. Berlin: Akademie-Verlag, 1964, pp. 97–112. A superficial analysis.

LANG, OLGA. *Pa Chin and His Writings: Chinese Youth Between The Two Revolutions*. Cambridge: Harvard University Press, 1967. Important study of Pa Chin's intellectual thought. Based on her doctoral dissertation.

―――. "Writer Pa Chin and His Time: Chinese Youth of the Transitional Period." Unpublished Ph.D. dissertation. Columbia University, 1962.

LECHOWSKA, T. "In Search of a New Ideal: The Metamorphoses of Pa Chin's Model Heroes." *ArOr*, 42 (1974), pp. 310–22. An interesting study of the ideals of some of Pa Chin's heroes whose idealism undergoes a continuous change as they move from the state of oppression to freedom.

―――. "Pa Chin" in *Dictionary of Oriental Literatures*, 3d. by Jaroslav Provek. New York: Basic Books, 1974. Vol. 1, pp. 135–36. A brief account of Pa Chin's life and work.

LEE, LEO OU-FAN. *The Romantic Generation of Modern Chinese Writers*. Cambridge: Harvard University Press, 1973. A brilliant study of several major Chinese writers.

LIN MAN-SHU et al. *Chung-kuo tang-tai tso-chia hsiao-ch'uan (Biographies D'Auteurs Chinois Contemporarins)*. Paris: Centre de publication Asie orientale de l'Université Paris 7, 1976, pp. 46–47. In Chinese, a very succinct account of Pa Chin's life, including a bibliography of secondary sources on Pa Chin and his works.

MAO, NATHAN K. "Pa Chin's Journey in Sentiment: From Hope to Despair," in *Journal of the Chinese Language Teachers Association*. Vol. XI, Number 2 (May 1975), pp. 131–37. Traces Pa Chin's growing pessimism.

―――, and LIU TS'UN-YAN, trs. *Cold Nights (Han-yeh)*. Hong Kong and Seattle: The Chinese University Press and The University of Washington Press, 1978. A literal translation.

MESERVE, WALTER, J., and MESERVE, RUTH I., eds. *Modern Drama from China*. New York: New York University Press, 1974. Contains selections of modern Chinese drama. Introduction sketchy.

MILLER, MARTIN A., ed. *Selected Writings on Anarchism and Revolution* by *Peter A. Kropotkin.* Cambridge: The MIT Press, 1970. Useful book on Kropotkin.

Ming-pao yüeh-k'an (Ming-pao Monthly). Vol. 10, Number 11 (November 1975), pp. 10–11. Reports on Pa Chin's nomination for the Nobel Prize in Literature.

MO CHIN-YI, tr. *Short Stories by Pa Chin, with English translations.* Hong Kong: Hui-t'ung shu-tien. Contains translations of "Fu-ch'ou" ("Revenge"); "Ch'u-lien" ("First Love"); and "Kou" ("Dog"). Identical with *Short Stories by Pa Chin,* ed. by Wen I. Shanghai: Chung-ying ch'u-pan she, 1941.

MONSTERLEET, JEAN. "La condition humaine dans *Chia (Famile)* de Pa Chin," in *Dossiers de la Commission Synodale* 15 (1942), pp. 578–99. Not seen.

――――. "Pakin 'Brumes,' " Doctorat d'Etat thesis complement, University of Paris, 1947. Not seen.

――――. "Pakin: Humanité Dieu or Homme Dieu," *China Missionary Bulletin* 6 (1950). Not seen.

――――. *Pa Chin ti sheng-huo ho chu-tso (Pa Chin's Life and Work).* Shanghai: Wen-feng ch'u-pan she, 1950. Analysis very superficial.

――――. "Pa Chin," *France Asie* 7.68 (Jan 1952), pp. 732–45.

――――. "Pa Kin," *Asia: Asian Quarterly of Culture and Synthesis,* 3.11 (December 1963), pp. 414–27.

――――. "Note sur Pa Chin et les Maitres qui l'ont Forme," *Revue de Litterature Comparée,* 28 (1954), pp. 89–92.

――――. "En Quete de Lumière et de Vie: Pa Chin, Un Romancier Chinois Moderne," in *Mission Bulletin* 8 (June 1956), pp. 406–11.

SHAPIRO, SIDNEY, tr. *The Family (Chia).* Peking: Foreign Languages Press, 1958. Reprinted by Doubleday and Co., Inc., 1972, with supplemental parts translated by Lu Kuang-huan and introduction by Olga Lang. An abridged translation.

――――. "A Moonlit Night" ("Yüeh-yeh") in *Chinese Literature,* 1962, No. 5, pp. 43–50.

SHENG, HSIEN, tr. "We Shall Always Stand Together" (Chinese title not given) in *Chinese Literature,* 1961, No. 8, pp. 41–47.

SHERIDAN, JAMES E. *China in Disintegration.* New York: The Free Press, 1975. A general introduction to modern China.

SNOW, EDGAR. *Living China: Modern Chinese Short Stories.* London: George G. Harper & Co., Ltd., 1936. Contains a translation of "Kou" ("Dog"), pp. 174–80.

――――. *Red Star Over China.* New York: Grove Press, 1968. Informative.

TANG, SHENG, tr. "When the Snow Melted" ("Hua-hsüeh ti jih-tzu") in *Chinese Literature,* 1962, No. 5, pp. 50–63.

TING-YI (YEH TING-YI). *A Short History of Modern Chinese Fiction.* New York: Kennikat Press, 1970. Useful for general reference.

WANG, C. C., tr. "The Puppet Dead" (Excerpt: Chapter 34 of *Family*) in

Wang's *Contemporary Chinese Stories*. New York: Columbia University Press, 1944, pp. 80–94. Excellent translation.

WANG, YAO. *Chung-kuo hsin wen-hsüeh shih-ko (A Draft History of Modern Chinese Literature)*. 2 volumes. Shanghai: Hsin wen-yi she, 1954. Biased but important.

WONG, BETTY. "Pa Chin in His Middle Period as a Novelist. An Analysis of Characters in the *Torrent Trilogy* and *Fire*." Unpublished M.A. Thesis. Columbia University, 1967. Critical of Pa Chin's writing techniques.

WONG, HARRIET, tr. "Dawn at Sea" ("Hai-shang ti jih-ch'u") in *Journal of Oriental Literature 2* (June 1948), p. 5.

YANG, C. K. *The Chinese Family in the Communist Revolution*. Cambridge: The MIT Press, 1959. Good, useful reference.

YEH, MUI SHANG-LAN, tr. "To a Cousin — Preface to the 10th edition of 'Family' " in *Renditions,* No. 4 (Spring 1975), pp. 73–82. Excellent.

YU, FAN-CHIN, tr. "Photographs from Kamakura" ("Tsung lien-ts'ang tai-hui ti chao-p'ien") in *Chinese Literature,* 1963, No. 6, pp. 62–67.

YÜ, SSU-MU. *Tso-chia Pa Chin (Writer Pa Chin)*. Hong Kong: Nan-kuo ch'u-pan she, 1964. Lots of summaries, weak analysis.

Index

The listing of books and article titles in the index is not exhaustive. Authors and titles appearing solely as references in Notes and References and in Bibliography are not included.

167